# Yes! GOD STILL SPEAKS Today

*Compiled by Norma Plank*

Christian Light Publications
Harrisonburg, Virginia 22802

YES! GOD STILL SPEAKS TODAY

Christian Light Publications, Inc.
Harrisonburg, Virginia 22802
© 2009 by Christian Light Publications, Inc.
Printed in the United States of America

2nd Printing, 2011


Cover design: Rhoda Miller


ISBN: 978-0-87813-669-8

928707

# Contents

# III.

## GOD SPEAKS THROUGH CIRCUMSTANCES

# IV.

## GOD SPEAKS THROUGH NATURE

# V.

## GOD SPEAKS THROUGH A STILL SMALL VOICE

# VI.

## GOD SPEAKS THROUGH
## STRONG PROMPTINGS

# VII.

## GOD SPEAKS THROUGH MIRACULOUS WAYS

# *Preface*

People have urged me to write some of my personal experiences, but I held back. Then one day I realized that many Christians have stories needing to be told, and in so doing, we could magnify the Lord together. I felt God urging me to solicit contributions for this book for the purpose of honoring and glorifying our great and mighty God. He alone is worthy of praise. I gave writers the privilege of changing names and locations for privacy if they wished, but one thing was required—stories must be true.

Yes, God still speaks today. Every true Christian knows this to be so. We also know He never speaks contrary to His Word, which will never change.

God is ever ready to help us in our times of need or to aid us in helping another needy person. At times, God's promptings may be foreign to our usual way of thinking.

God uses various means to speak to us:

1. Through His Word
2. Through ministers, parents, and Christian brothers and sisters
3. Through circumstances
4. Through nature
5. Through a still small voice and conscience

6. Through strong promptings

7. Through miraculous ways.

Every contributor willingly and humbly shared personal experiences. Only a few changed names or locations.

I was thrilled to receive permission to write about some happenings that took place in North Korea and China. I credit Cornerstone Ministries International for these contributions.

I want to thank Mrs. Steven (Lydia) Good and Nelson and Florence Heatwole, who generously took time to read and to do some editing on this book. I greatly appreciate the many people who encouraged me during the compilation and editorial work.

It is our desire that this book will help to build a greater faith and confidence in our all-powerful God and to help us have a listening ear, eager to hear Him. Loving, wholehearted submission to the heavenly Father's will is the key to having our spiritual ears open to hear the voice of the Holy Spirit, who desires to speak to us and to direct our paths.

### *Our God is Great!*

### *The Holy Spirit is still working through His Faithful Ones.*

### *Praise His Holy Name!*

# I.

GOD SPEAKS THROUGH HIS

*Word*

# 1

## God's Precious Word

*Norma Plank*
*Rewritten by permission*

Though the enemy hinders, God always increases the boundaries of His Kingdom.

In late July of 2002, I was traveling with an intercessory team in China. Stopping by a small house church, we asked if we could join the Chinese Christians during their worship service. They replied that, since we were foreigners, we could not. They were afraid that the Public Security Bureau would discover their gathering.

"If that's the case," we replied, "could we use your home and worship by ourselves?"

They just looked at us and shook their heads.

As we turned to leave, one of our team said, "We brought Bibles. Do you need any?"

The leader's eyes suddenly grew large. "Chinese Bibles?" he asked.

"Yes," we replied.

Then an old man, who looked to be seventy years old, stood up. "We have been praying for Bibles for twenty years," he said, with tears streaming down his face. "We have only one Bible, which we share among the thirty of us who meet here."

You should have seen their faces as we went through our sacks and presented them with thirty Chinese Bibles. They were more joyful than children on Christmas morning. We cried with them as they reverently took the precious Word of God into their hands.

So, we worshiped with them after all! What a blessed fellowship it was! What a privilege!

# 2

# Not My Will, But Thine

*Wilma Hofer*

At the doctor's office I met a woman who is blind because of diabetes. It caused me to think, *Lord, forgive me when I complain; I have two good eyes.* Others were there in wheelchairs. Again I thought, *I'm in my seventies, but I can walk as much as two miles for my daily exercise. How blessed I am! Thank You, Lord.*

I came home with a grateful heart, so I should have been better prepared for what followed that evening—an opportunity to gracefully adjust my plans in order to help a bedfast sister.

Earlier I had agreed to go with Verna to help Bertha the next week. Bertha is a dear bedfast sister in our church. Her husband was recently reinstated as a member, which brings her great joy. They have ten children, but none live nearby. Sometimes they come and help care for their mother. Bertha could move closer to them, but for her spiritual well-being, she wants to live near her church family.

The phone rang. Julia wondered if I would go with her to help Bertha *this* week. I thought, *This week and next week too?*

I said, "I can't; that's my shopping day."

Unknown to me, Julia called the preacher's wife, but she had a full schedule and wasn't available. Then the preacher's wife called me. "Will you go with Julia to care for Bertha?" she asked. "I just can't go this time."

By this time, I wasn't feeling very happy. I didn't want my shopping plans spoiled, but God was speaking to me through His Word. "Inasmuch as ye have done it unto one of the least of these . . . , ye have done it unto me" (Matthew 25:40).

"Yes, Lord," I answered Him, "I do want to do that, but not tomorrow morning."

I'm happy to say I repented of my wrong feelings and for wondering why others couldn't do more for this dear sister.

Home-care nurses come and bathe Bertha, but she also has other needs, and she enjoys the fellowship of her Christian sisters. Bertha's mind is very good. She's a blessing to visit with. I can't imagine what it would be like to be in her place, unable to move in bed, unable even to wipe my own tears.

So, Julia will come soon to pick me up, and I can say that I go willingly and the Lord has graciously forgiven me. Yes, some of my plans, including my daily nap, are placed on the back burner. But that's all right, for I know the Lord will give me grace as I willingly and lovingly submit to His will. I need to learn to focus more on what the Lord wants me to do today and not to be disturbed when my carefully planned days are interrupted.

*O LORD, I know that the way of man is not in himself:*
*it is not in man that walketh to direct his steps.*
Jeremiah 10:23

# 3

# I Will Go in the Strength of the Lord

*Vilas Amstutz*

Life for me began on a farm in Ohio in 1925. At age fourteen, I accepted the Lord as my Savior. When World War II came and the draft registration began, I applied for conscientious objector status. I was deferred to the home farm for one year, and then the draft board transferred me to a larger farm where the farmer had only one arm. After the war was over and all the CPS (Civilian Public Service) men and drafted soldiers were home again, I went to work on an uncle's farm. It was during this time I made a new commitment and rededicated my life to the Lord.

Since I hadn't served in CPS, I wanted to do some voluntary service. At a six-week winter Bible school I was introduced to Nelson Kauffman of the Hannibal Mennonite Mission in Hannibal, Missouri. He said they needed a handyman at the mission because he was often away in church work.

Could the Lord possibly want someone like me to serve in such a place? Someone who had only eight years of schooling? Was He asking me to serve in a city mission when I knew nothing but farming? This was beyond my comprehension. I shared my burden with a friend who met with me numerous times in the prayer room.

One day the Lord spoke to my heart as I read Psalm 71:16. "I will go in the strength of the Lord GOD: I will make mention of thy righteousness, even of thine only." This verse gave me the courage to say "yes" to this opportunity.

About a month later, I was on the train, going west— farther than I had ever been. In Hannibal I served as janitor, drove the church bus, visited people in the community, taught Sunday school and summer Bible school, and took Brother Kauffman to distant train stations or picked him up on his way home.

It was here that I met my wife-to-be, Lillian Brunk, who was Brother Kauffman's secretary. She was from a different part of Ohio. After we married, we continued to live in Hannibal another fifteen months. Lillian's mother had died and her youngest sister was keeping house for their father. Due to the sister's illness and the urging of my wife's family, we moved home to keep house for Lillian's father.

We attended and served at Lillian's home church for eight years, after which the church appointed us to serve at an outreach mission eight miles away where we served for nearly thirty years. We felt God was speaking and leading us through these various circumstances in life.

The Lord gave us the joy of adopting, on the same day, three little sisters aged three, five, and seven. Our cup of joy was full and running over.

Psalms 71:16 has been a source of encouragement throughout my life. "I will go in the strength of the Lord GOD: I will make mention of thy righteousness, even of thine only."

# 4

## *His Promise Is True*

*Wilma Hofer*

When I was sixty-five and a widow for two years, a school board member knocked on my door in the person of my son Paul, the oldest of my ten children.

He made a startling request. "Would you consider teaching the elementary classes after Christmas? Our present teacher is scheduled for surgery in January."

My thoughts began to spin. *Me? A teacher at sixty-five? Sure, in my youth I had longed for the opportunity to teach, but there were no Christian day schools then. I enjoyed teaching summer Bible school and Sunday school, and I have taught my ten children. But now? At my age?*

The Lord spoke to my heart from a verse in Exodus 33:14. "My presence shall go with thee, and I will give thee rest."

Israel had forsaken God and worshiped the golden calf as the god that delivered them from slavery. After Moses had dealt with Aaron and the people, he went back up the mountain and begged the Lord to forgive their great sin and to go with them. God did forgive them, but Moses needed God's presence also; he could not walk this untried path alone.

Then God assured him with these wonderful words, "My presence shall go with thee, and I will give thee rest."

That promise was enough for me too; I accepted the challenge—placing my faith in His promise.

The school board provided me with good help, but the responsibility was mine. Some challenging problems arose. I had four grandchildren in my room, and although I tried to be fair, this sometimes posed a problem. Added to this were some pupil and parent difficulties. I knew some parents were unhappy with the school board's choice for a substitute teacher. So, I had reason to remember this verse each day; I needed the assurance of His presence.

Improvements were made, but the problems couldn't be completely solved. It was only by God's grace and strength that I could continue on.

There were days when I began to feel like Moses when he struck the rock, *Here now, ye rebels, must I try to teach you something?* But my reason for aggravation was nothing when I compared it to all Moses had to face. Often I needed to ask the Lord to please forgive my wrong attitudes and to give me a meek and quiet spirit.

It was humbling, because when I lashed out with angry words, I needed to ask forgiveness and ask for His help to control my reactions. This was a growing time in walking with my Lord. I was able to say, "Thank You, Lord, for the hard times; these have been good for my soul and caused me to look to You."

Also I needed to remind myself of this: *Who am I that I need to be treated with love and respect? They didn't show love and respect to my Lord on Calvary, and He even said, "Father, forgive them, for they know not what they do."*

Even after the school year was over, I felt like avoiding the people with whom there had been difficulties until I realized that was not right. I needed to return good to them, so I tried to follow the Bible way.

Some years later, I realized the strained relationships had changed! What joy filled my heart! How I thanked the Lord! He had given me rest.

I had learned that sometimes He bids us have patience and wait, knowing He is there even in our waiting times. If we continue to trust Him, He will give us rest even while we wait.

# 5

## The Father Gives Direction

*Carolyn Roth*

*The sophomore slump!* Two more years to go! How could I bear another two years in academia? I began investigating opportunities to teach in church schools and prayed that God would open up a job for me in the fall.

Spring . . . summer . . . mid-August . . . I had to make some decisions. One morning I prayed desperately for direction and searched the Word for an answer. What was I to do? Reading in Jeremiah, I suddenly found God's *rhema* for me! "Why gaddest thou about so much to change thy way?" (Jeremiah 2:36).

*Why indeed?* I had felt God's leading to go to college, to prepare for teaching, so now why was I second-guessing His guidance? I did not need to change my way. He gave me peace to stay where I was and to stop fretting about the teaching job. My heavenly Father would show me if He wanted me to make a change.

About a week later, the director of Northern Light Gospel Missions called to ask if I would consider teaching in their Development School at Poplar Hill. A last-minute change had left them without a primary teacher and school was to begin the following week. Immediately I knew why God had closed all other doors for teaching jobs. He wanted me in Northern Ontario! My parents' approval confirmed God's peace within, and off I went for three life-changing years.

# Age Doesn't Count

*Norma Plank*

Let us never underestimate the value of the printed
page and the convicting power of God's Word.

When I was in my early teens, our church distributed a
tract called *The Way* once a month. Our pastor's name
and address was stamped on the back of the tract. Very
early on Sunday mornings we placed the tracts by each
door close to the morning newspaper, where it would be
easily found. We always went by twos—each taking opposite sides of the street, but keeping a watchful eye for any
trouble the other might encounter.

As we passed out tracts one frosty Sunday morning, we
approached a railroad crossing. Next to the crossing sat a
big steam engine. The engineer looked out his window
and waved. I held out a tract, and he nodded and reached
out his hand invitingly. I rushed forward. He leaned
down from his cab and I, on tiptoe, reached up as high as
I could to hand him the tract. We exchanged no conversation because of the noisy engine, which was "chuffing"

and now and then blowing clouds of steam and smoke into the chilly air.

Seldom do we hear the results that tracts have on people's lives, but God saw fit to thrill me with the result of handing out this tract.

Several weeks later my pastor approached me after church. "Norma," he said, "I want you to know that you were instrumental in helping a soul find the Lord."

"Who, me?" I was wide-eyed with surprise.

"Yes," my minister said. "I received a letter from a railroad engineer. In his letter he described a young girl, which has to be you. He said you handed him a tract and after reading it, he was converted. He asked me to pass the good news on to you."

I could hardly believe my ears. The Lord had used me, even if I was young. I realized then that age doesn't count. All He needs is a heart that's willing to do what He wants. And it wasn't me, but the Word of God that had spoken to the engineer's heart; I was only God's instrument to pass the Word into the engineer's hand.

Many people do not go to church or listen to any kind of gospel witness. But God's Spirit can work silently through an attractive, well-written tract left in a public phone booth, motel room, or restaurant, reaching people who will read them only when alone. Without tracts, some people may never hear.

# 7

## The Lord's Battle

*Martha B. (Yoder) Shank*

"What do you mean? Why do I need more x-rays?" I exclaimed, suddenly aware of what the doctor was saying.

"We see a small mass in your right breast, and we need to get a more detailed study," the doctor explained kindly. "We'll set up the appointment and call you."

On the way home I had troubled thoughts. *I'm facing a battle. It's probably cancer. Maybe I'll not fight it and just die! It's too hard to live with all our problems anyway. This will take me out of my misery.* I was sinking into a familiar pattern of depression.

When I arrived home, I happened to glance at the calendar. I gasped. "Oh no, I'm scheduled to have children's class tonight at church. Well, I'll just grit my teeth and do my duty. I can use the lesson from 2 Chronicles 20 that I used two years ago."

Usually I enjoyed my turn with my little friends, but this night I felt dull. I asked the children, "Do you remember the song I taught you the last time we had class together?" They remembered, and we sang, *My Lord knows the way through the wilderness, All I have to do is follow*. After singing it twice, the words pricked my heart.

Unenthusiastically, I began telling the story. "Tonight I want to tell you about King Jehoshaphat. He was really worried. Three countries were planning to make war with him. What was he to do? He was afraid and set himself to seek the Lord. He called his people together to ask for help from the Lord. Together they fasted and prayed. The king prayed, and here is one thing he said: 'Neither know we what to do, but our eyes are on Thee.' "

I repeated this prayer several times. *Was that God talking to me through this?*

"Then a prophet, a man of God, came to Jehoshaphat telling him, 'The battle is not yours, but it is God's.'

"The king was surprised. He began praising God with a loud voice for this message."

As I repeated these words from the Bible, I sensed God's blessing coming to my own heart.

I began speaking with enthusiasm. "In the morning the king instructed all his singers to march in the front lines and his army to follow behind. With rejoicing, the king ordered, 'As we go toward the enemy, I want you to sing, "Praise the Lord, for his mercy endureth forever." The Lord will go with you and He will fight our battle for us.'

"When they arrived where they could see the enemy, they gasped. Every one of their enemies was lying dead on the ground. Indeed, it was God's battle just as He had promised. What a great God He is!"

*What a great God He is!* I exclaimed from the depth of my own heart.

As I reviewed the story with the children, I was pleased with how much the children had grasped.

But I knew the Lord had used this lesson to bless me with His peace and rest. I realized anew that the future of all things, even my health, was in the Lord's hands. The battle of my life was the Lord's. I left the classroom with a song of victory in my heart.

# Yes, God Forgives

*Ruth (Martin) Groff*
*As told to Norma Plank*

Ruth Martin was alone in her house. A widow, she often talked aloud to her heavenly Father, and today was no exception. Ruth was grieving. She had sinned.

A godly sorrow caused her to cry out from a full heart. "Please, dear Father, forgive me; make me clean." Then looking up as though the Lord was visible, she said, "I know You have forgiven me, Lord, but please, let me hear it in an audible voice."

Ruth dropped to her knees by the end of the couch and opened her Bible in front of her. It fell open to 2 Corinthians 7 where she began reading aloud, "Having therefore these promises, dearly beloved, let us cleanse ourselves from all filthiness of the flesh and spirit, perfecting holiness in the fear of God."

Deeply blessed, she continued reading through the chapter. When she got to the 11th verse, her heart sang with joy. God had answered her request to hear Him say in an audible voice that He had forgiven her—her voice as she read! The verse said, "For behold this selfsame thing, that ye sorrowed after a godly sort, what carefulness it wrought in you, yea, what clearing of yourselves, yea, what indignation, yea, what fear, yea, what vehement desire, yea, what zeal, yea, what revenge! In all things ye have approved yourselves to be clear in this matter."

Ruth's heart bubbled over with joy; she had peace; the matter was settled. God had forgiven! And He had spoken through His Word in an audible voice.

# The Purpose for Living

*Janelle Tudor*

*There's no place to turn!* thought Joan. *Why, oh, why, is there no light? There is no way to go on!* Joan was caught into the depths of depression. She felt pushed against a stone wall with no way to get beyond it.

*I must die! I can't live! There's no way to go on!* echoed over and over in her weakened mind. It became an obsession to her. She was oblivious to the truth that her loving husband Isaac cared deeply for her. But he felt unable to reach her, because Joan had allowed herself to sink into a pit of depression, shutting herself off from his love. Nor did she call for the help of her loving heavenly Father who saw her great need.

Joan functioned like a robot as she prepared meals for her husband and children, washed clothes, and did the household chores. All the while, she was overwhelmed with the obsession, *I must die! I can't go on living!*

One afternoon Isaac, with a heavy heart, prepared to leave for work. As he leaned down to kiss Joan good-bye, she looked up at him coldly from some dark corner of her depressed mind. "That's the last kiss you'll ever get," she warned.

Isaac knew those words were an urgent cry for help. He could not leave his wife at home alone.

Trembling, he dialed his boss. "I'm unable to come to work today. My wife is terribly sick."

Hanging up the phone, Isaac sank onto the couch and burst into tears. Joan sat, numb and unfeeling.

Gradually composing himself, and with a silent prayer to his Lord, he again dialed the phone—this time for Dr. King. "I need help right now for Joan!" he begged the receptionist.

Dr. King knew what Isaac meant because several days before Joan had been at the local hospital. The treatment had not helped.

"Isaac, please get someone to go with you yet today and take Joan to the Christian Psychiatric Hospital in Johnstown. I'll call there immediately."

Dr. King's firm response brought a thread of relief. Isaac knew his wife could no longer be trusted alone. This was not his formerly pleasant wife, but one who had become very unbalanced in her thinking. He could hardly imagine taking her so far from home, but she needed help, and he did too.

In a short time Dr. King called back. "Have Joan there before bedtime tonight," he said. "They are expecting her. And Isaac, I will join you in prayer for her healing. We know this is not our usual Joan. She needs help."

Isaac immediately called Pastor Hoover. "I need to take Joan to a hospital yet tonight. Can you get someone to go with us?"

"My wife and I will take you, Isaac," comforted Pastor Hoover. "Give us two hours to arrange things. And we'll ask someone to take care of your children overnight."

Joan had heard Isaac making the phone calls. She felt no embarrassment or other reaction—she was emotionally numb.

Isaac turned to his wife and said, "Joan, I need your help. Pastor Hoover and his wife are coming in two hours to take us to the hospital. Dr. King feels you'll get the help you need there. Now, you must get ready to go, and you'll be staying for awhile. You also need to help me get clothes together for the children to stay overnight with someone. Pastor Hoover is making arrangements."

As Isaac helped a sullen Joan to her feet, he was so thankful there had been someone to call on for help. Their children had been picked up by another church family before Pastor Hoover and his wife arrived. Soon Isaac and Joan were in the back seat of their pastor's car, heading to the hospital.

Those first weeks were a stormy, painful experience for Joan. One day, after repeated counseling sessions with her Christian doctor, she left his office and for the first time went to the prayer room.

Lying face down on the floor in distress, she cried in anguish, "O Lord, I don't know how I got into this mess, neither do I know how to get out of this mess! O Lord, forgive me. I surrender this whole situation to You."

As she prayed this, it seemed as if she were standing by an endless swinging bridge with no handholds, and she knew she had to cross that bridge. Her old ways of thinking and functioning, her reactions to hurts, were slopping up between the floorboards to pull her back into it again. But she had to cross that bridge!

*This must be the way a drug addict feels when he accepts Jesus and knows he is a new creature and not wanting to go back to his former life,* thought Joan.

She sobbed as she told one of the counselors her experience. "I can't go, I don't know how, I'm so afraid."

Quietly he comforted her. "We are here to help you, Joan. We will help you every step we can. And our heavenly Father is here to help you every moment. Let's pray right now."

The next morning these words were in Joan's mind. "Choose life! Choose life!" *That sounds like Scripture,* she thought. Using her concordance she found the verse was Deuteronomy 30:19. "I call heaven and earth to record this day against you, that I have set before you life and death, blessing and cursing: therefore choose life, that both thou and thy seed may live."

"Thank You, Lord! You are giving me the desire to live! Oh, thank You, God!" cried Joan.

In her excitement, she read further, "That thou mayest love the LORD thy God, and that thou mayest obey his voice, and that thou mayest cleave unto him: for he is thy life, and the length of thy days."

"God, forgive me! I cannot take my own life. That is in Your hands. The length of my life here on earth is in Your hand and must never be in mine." Joan's prayer was filled with a joy she had not known for a long time.

Joan rejoiced in this Spirit-filled moment, but her healing came slowly. She frequently remembered her vision of the swinging bridge. Finally, she sensed Jesus was carrying her across the bridge, but it seemed as though even Jesus was shaking at His knees. She shared her thoughts with her counselor.

"Is your God too small, Joan?" he questioned. From his well-worn Bible, he read to her of the greatness of God.

Then came the day when Joan knew she was on the Rock. That day the vision of the bridge disappeared, and her heart rejoiced, "My feet are on the Rock now and the bridge is gone. All praise to God!"

One helper opened her Bible and read, "I waited patiently for the LORD; and he inclined unto me, and heard my cry. He brought me up also out of an horrible pit, out of the miry clay, and set my feet upon a rock, and established my goings" (Psalm 40:1, 2).

"That's me! That's what happened!" Joan exclaimed in wonder at how the Psalmist had had such a similar experience and could put it into words for her.

The Lord was with Joan through this "pit" experience, and though there were times she again fell into emotional disturbances, yet she was not utterly cast down, for the Lord held her with His hand. She claimed the promises for His keeping power.

# 10

## An Urgent Eleven O'Clock Call

*Waneta Sandlin*
*As told to Norma Plank*

One night while working a 3-to-11 shift at a nursing home in Lima, Ohio, I received an urgent call from my daughter-in-law. "My grandfather is dying," she cried, "and I'm not sure he is saved. Would you come to the hospital and talk to him?"

I thought, *I hardly know the man and furthermore, I'm a woman.* I thought of Moses' words in the Bible, " 'I am not eloquent . . . but I am slow of speech and and of a slow tongue.' And the LORD said, 'Who hath made man's mouth . . . ? Have not I, the LORD? Now therefore go, and I will be with thy mouth, and teach thee what thou shalt say.' "

I suggested several ministers, but for some reason they didn't work out. Next, I suggested the hospital chaplain. My daughter-in-law said she had tried, but he was gone and would not be back until in the morning. She was afraid her grandfather wouldn't live that long.

I thought, *Lord, what am I to do?*

The Lord said, "You must go."

My daughter-in-law picked me up at the end of my shift, 11:00 p.m.

I said, "Lord, what am I to say? You will have to give me the words."

I knew my daughter-in-law's father was not a church-going man, and it was his father who was dying, so I asked her, "Do you think your dad will care if I come and talk to his dad?"

She said, "No, it's all right with him."

My daughter-in-law asked a lot of questions while we drove to the hospital. One question was, "Could Grand-father be saved since he is so near the end of his life?"

I assured her that he could and reminded her that sal-vation was extended to one of the thieves hanging on the cross beside Jesus. Then I said, "But it is dangerous to put off getting saved until the eleventh hour, because we have no promise that we will have that chance."

When we walked into her grandfather's hospital room, it was clear he was very near death's door. I am not sure he even knew I was there, but I went ahead and explained the way of salvation and prayed with him. I had heard that people in a coma can sometimes hear but can't respond verbally.

By the next morning the man had died. I was so glad I heeded the call and with God's help did what I could.

# II.

GOD SPEAKS THROUGH HIS

*People*

# 11

## "Be Not Deceived"

*Names changed for privacy  Anonymous*

When I was a little schoolgirl, I dreamed of getting married someday and having a family. My school chums and I would play "house" and "church." Some of my classmates would make remarks such as, "I'm never going to get married." Even then I knew my heart's desire, so I never made such a statement.

Years passed and I watched those classmates start dating, followed by marriage and children. I had some dates, but never felt the Lord saying, "This is the one." I never lost my desire to have a home and family of my own, but I wanted to be sure God was leading.

In my thirties I became good friends with Rachel, a non-Mennonite widow. Rachel's daughter Nettie was married and had three children. Quite often they asked me to babysit them.

Rachel had a married son, Martin, who lived in another state with his wife Donna and two little girls, Sally (2½ years) and Hope (4 months).

Eventually Martin moved his family closer to his mother Rachel and sister Nettie. Martin's wife had become abusive to her husband, but when she began abusing the girls, Martin sought a divorce. The judge gave him custody of the little girls. When their mother would come to pick up the girls for visitation, Sally fearfully clung to her daddy, begging to stay with him. It was heartrending, but according to the law she had to go.

Martin had come to know the Lord and spent time fasting and praying for his little girls. I was asked to babysit for Martin's children along with Nettie's children. It was obvious that little Sally and Hope were being taught about the Lord. Their sweetness worked its way right to the center of my heart.

For several years I continued babysitting and helping in other ways with Nettie's and Martin's children. I began thinking of Sally and Hope as "my girls." And before long I began questioning what I had been taught about divorce and remarriage. Legally, Martin was single and free to remarry. The law was clear on that point, but I had been taught that as long as Donna lived, Martin was not free to remarry.

I turned a deaf ear to my conscience and began reasoning, *After all, Martin is a good Christian man and many churches would say he is free to remarry. Maybe the Mennonite church isn't correct on this teaching.* I became very confused. I lost my peace with God as I allowed myself to begin loving this man. I refused to listen to the still small voice of God.

I was thrilled when Martin began paying attention to me in a romantic way. I remember so well one day when I was with him, I felt I was in Satan's trap, but I was not willing to walk away. If only I had walked away, the rest of this story would be different.

Time and again Martin would ask me to meet him somewhere, and for a long time I stood firm and said, "No." Then I began to weaken as I argued with myself. *Maybe our church is wrong on this issue. Maybe it isn't really sin. After all, a lot of churches teach that it's all right. Oh, who is right?* I was miserable, but unwilling to give Martin up.

Besides babysitting, I was also doing some house cleaning jobs. One of my jobs was located forty-five minutes away. I finally agreed to meet Martin there for lunch. It seemed far enough from home that my family would not find out. This was the first of many secret meetings with him for lunch. A few times he brought his two little girls along. They made it clear they wanted a mother who loved them. Someone gave Sally a ring, which she gave to her daddy, telling him he should give it to me so I could be her mother.

Yes, I did love those little girls, and I longed to be their mother. Yes, Martin wanted to marry me, and I wanted to marry him. I was caught up in the thrill of being special to someone. I no longer knew what to believe and doubted my understanding of Scripture. I even went to our minister and his wife and questioned them on the verse in Matthew 5:32, "But I say unto you, That whosoever shall put away his wife, saving for the cause of fornication, causeth her to commit adultery: and whosoever shall marry her that is divorced committeth adultery."

A terrible war was raging in my heart. Though many thoughts whirled through my mind, the one that was uppermost was something my dear, godly mother had told her seven children. "There is one thing," she said, "that scares me more than any persecution my children might endure, and that is deception. I'm praying that none of my children will be deceived." The thought of being deceived scared me, and those words came to my mind many times.

According to what I was taught, I could not marry Martin while Donna was alive. Neither did I want her to die and meet the Lord in her sinful condition. My wishful imaginations carried me away in thinking that maybe Donna would give her heart to God and then He would take her home, leaving Martin free to marry me. One day, while traveling, I listened to a gospel message. The minister talked about Haman and how he died on the gallows he had built for another person. I did not want my thought life to boomerang and end my life, so I did not dwell on that thought anymore.

During this time I took part in several Communion services. I knew it was wrong to partake of Communion while I had sin in my life. One time I refrained from taking Communion. The other times I asked God to forgive me, and I told Martin I was sorry and could no longer see him. Afterward the tempter would come again, and I would think maybe Martin was right, and I would agree to meet him again.

When my family finally learned that Martin and I had a deeper relationship than just being a baby sitter or friend, they were shocked. They could hardly believe I was so blind to the dangers. I loved my family and didn't want to hurt them, but I also loved Martin.

One time Martin invited me to his and Nettie's church for a Christmas program. All five of their children were in the children's choir and Martin was in the adult choir. I accepted the invitation and took a small tape recorder along and recorded the singing. This tape was very special to me and often I would take it along to work and listen to the singing. While listening to this tape during one of our "off" times when we were not seeing each other, I was overcome with terrible grief as I realized they were singing praises to God, and I was not a part of their family. I cried so hard I became sick at my stomach. At that point, I decided this was enough and threw the tape in the trash. But sad to say, I later agreed on another lunch date.

In my home church we had one night a month called "Family Night." When it was our family's turn to plan the program, we asked my uncle to come and give a sermon. I always enjoyed hearing my uncle preach, because he preached with such deep conviction. I was glad he didn't know I was having a spiritual battle about divorce and remarriage, because I was sure of his stand.

My uncle agreed to come and preach on the importance of having convictions. He had not planned to mention any specific area of conviction, but felt the Lord was pressing on him to say something about divorce and remarriage. So for the next few minutes he spoke directly on the very thing I was battling with; and I sat there and squirmed.

As time went on, Martin could see I was really struggling. He decided to put his own desires aside. He encouraged me to mind the Lord and do what I needed to do, so I could have peace with God. He said he knew, on the Day of Judgment, we must all stand before God on our own and he wanted me to have peace. His kindness and concern tore at my heart, but I appreciated it.

I was tired and weary of trying to figure out if we as Mennonites were wrong or right in our understanding of scripture. One night I cried out to the Lord to show me what to do.

I closed my eyes and tried to visualize myself standing before God on the judgment day after having married Martin. Suddenly, I felt myself trembling with fear. Then I tried to visualize myself standing before God on the judgment day after having said "no" to Martin and the song "Oh, Victory in Jesus" rang in my head.

I said, "Lord, I'll accept this by faith and never question the matter again. Just help me to rest in You for the present, and please clear up my confusion and give me firm convictions of my own—based on Your Word."

Years later, I told my uncle that I was the reason the Lord wanted him to preach that night on divorce and remarriage. Though he had found out later about my involvement, at the time he knew nothing.

Satan knew my weak points and tried to drive in a wedge wherever he could; but I'm so thankful the Lord was willing to pick me up, and I could go on again in victory.

Several years have passed, and I am happy to say I have firm convictions that it is Bible truth not to marry a divorced person as long as their spouse is still living. The Bible is clear that marrying a divorced person while their spouse is living is adultery. Unless the sin of adultery is confessed and forsaken, it will take one straight to hell.

> *Be not deceived: neither fornicators, . . . nor*
> *adulterers, . . . shall inherit the kingdom of God.*
> 1 Corinthians 6:9, 10

# God Gave Me Assurance

*Waneta Sandlin*
*As told to Norma Plank*

Our church at Elida, Ohio, had asked the Ezra Good family to serve at a mission called Newfound, way back in the hills of Kentucky. To get to Newfound, you had three choices of travel—mule-back, walking, or a four-wheel-drive jeep. Mail delivery was by mule. Cars were unable to travel those rough roads, many of which ran right up the rocky creek beds.

Now and then a traveler would maneuver his jeep out of the creek to slip and slide along in the deep clay-mud ruts. Driving in the ruts had a safety benefit, because the narrow roads had no guardrails. Careless drivers who got out of the ruts could slide over the edge of any one of the many sheer drop-offs and crash into a deep ravine. Meeting another vehicle was rare, which was a good thing, since there were few places wide enough for passing.

Soon after the Good family left for Kentucky, our church asked for a woman volunteer to help in Brother Ezra and Sister Vida's home so they would be more free to visit in the community. During the service when the request was announced, I felt the Lord was asking me to serve in this difficult place, but I wasn't excited about the idea.

*They have no decent roads, no electricity, no phones, and no running water,* I thought. *Baths are taken from a pan or a washtub of water. And the people are so different; they let their pigs and chickens wander into their homes to pick up the food scraps on the floor around their tables. And they talk different too. I don't want to, Lord. Maybe You're not even asking me to go; maybe it is just my imagination. And besides, Lord, I'm already busy in Your work right here in Lima.*

Our church worked with black children in Victory Village, a community that had sprung up during World War II. It was made up of many poor, quickly-built shacks where people lived who worked in the war plants.

After the church service, I was surprised when Lola Brunk walked up to me and said, "Waneta, do you feel the Lord is asking you to go to Newfound, Kentucky, to help Brother Ezra's?"

I bowed my head and heart and said, "Yes, I feel the Lord is asking me to go. With you coming and asking me this question, I know God is confirming His will for me.

Please pray that God will make me willing, because I'd rather stay here."

I didn't need to tell the ministry; they came to me. "Waneta, would you be willing to go and help in the work at Newfound, Kentucky?"

So, at age twenty, I left for Newfound. I was glad for the assurance that God had called me. This assurance helped me through many difficult experiences.

# 13

# "Help! I'm Not Ready to Die"

*Leonard Shank*
*Names changed for privacy*

In August 1997, I started hauling U.S. mail to a distribution hub in another state, where about 250 people worked under nearly 30 Postal Service overseers.

Because this work is time-sensitive, it became very frustrating at times, causing temper eruptions and shouting confrontations. The biggest contentions occurred when a truck was held past regular dispatch time. With legal restrictions on the number of driving hours, most truckers were on a tight schedule to meet a relay driver who would hurry the mail on to its destination. A delayed dispatch meant a delay for the relay driver, and then, of course, the mail would arrive late.

Charlie and Sue began working there soon after I started delivering mail to this hub. I learned to know

Charlie, but I had more contact with Sue, because she was indirectly responsible for some facets of transportation.

Unknown to me, God was speaking to Sue while she watched my actions and reactions and made judgments about my spirituality. Sue noticed that each morning I was there, I chose a quiet corner in the break room and had a men's Bible study and prayer time with those who wished to attend. Whenever I realized one of the men was going through a crisis or family problem, I prayed for him right then. By earnestly praying for them and presenting God's Word, I could give these men direction and comfort.

Reflecting back, I remember Sue watching my reaction to someone's outburst over a delayed dispatch. I always tried to stay neutral because, regardless of the shouting and tempers, the work still had to be done—whether fair or not. I remember several times when Sue held my load for a late mail sort, but I tried not to let it bother me, even though it made my load late. We did get a "Late Dispatch" form, which meant that drivers did not have to speed to make up time on the road. I would always notify my relay driver when I would be late.

In October of 2003 I was alone in the break room on my regular layover developing a topic to give at church. My Bible and a couple other books were open on the table when Sue walked in. She stopped, took in my setup on the table, and without a word, walked to the other side of the room for a cup of coffee.

Carrying her coffee, she returned to my table and, uninvited, pulled out a chair and sat down. "Mr. Shank, I must talk to you!" she said.

"Okay," I replied and gave her my full attention.

"Mr. Shank, I have observed you for several years; you are different, and I think you can help me. Yesterday I was diagnosed with cancer—the same kind that killed my mother. I'm scared," she said, her voice breaking. "I'm not ready to die. Will you help me?"

*Okay, Lord,* I prayed quickly. *You promised to give me the words I need. I need them now!* Aloud, I said, "Sure, Sue, I will be glad to help all I can, but you know it is only God who can give you real help and peace."

Here sat a U. S. Postal employee on U. S. Postal property asking me to witness to her about God. Sue was very, very serious. I talked to her about her past, her marriage relationship, her past relationship with the Lord and the church, some sin issues that troubled her, and other matters. I determined that Sue was straightforward with me about these things and had come clean. Normally I lead someone to the Lord over several meetings, discussing Scripture and personal issues and giving ample time to think things over. But Sue wanted help immediately.

She had been raised in a church much like my own and was keenly aware of what was required of her. Some time during our discussion, her husband Charlie entered and joined us at the table.

Sue had many questions—intelligent, searching questions—and made several very thoughtful statements, some of them in Charlie's presence. It was obvious that Sue was ready; she understood the complete plan of salvation, and she confessed her need of the Lord Jesus.

"Sue, do really believe Jesus died for you and can forgive *all* your sins?" I asked.

She quickly replied, "Yes!"

Turning to Charlie I asked, "How about you, Charlie?"

"Go ahead with Sue," he said. "I'm not sure just what I believe. I'm too stressed out right now to think straight."

"Okay, Charlie, but will you support Sue and not hinder her or discourage her in this decision?"

"It's up to her whatever she decides; I won't stand in her way," promised Charlie.

"Charlie, Sue wants me to help her, so I'm going to help her invite Jesus into her life. I really would like for you to join her, but if you are not really convinced and ready, I will not pressure you, but I want you to stay with us while Sue and I approach God. Will you do that?"

"Okay," agreed Charlie.

I turned to Sue. "If you want Jesus to come into your life and abide with you through the trials ahead and for the remainder of your life, will you pray after me?"

"Yes," agreed Sue.

Together we prayed, "Dear Lord, I acknowledge I am a sinner and need Your forgiveness. I know without Your forgiveness I face Your judgment and eternal death. I believe You love me and showed Your love by sending Your Son Jesus Christ to die for my sins. I trust in this alone to put me in a right relationship with You. I ask You to take over my life and live within me. I know I am not worthy of this, but I thank You for it. In Jesus' name I pray. Amen."

As soon as we finished, a weeping Sue pled with Charlie to have me pray this prayer with him, but Charlie insisted he was not ready, and Sue's weeping and pleading did not change his mind.

A few days later, Sue started chemotherapy treatments and was off work for several months. I saw her only once after our experience in the break room. In early December, she stopped in to see some of her friends. She was happy in the Lord and had a joyful outlook.

"I have turned it all over to the Lord, and feel relaxed and at peace," she said. "Charlie and I have started attending the church you suggested. The pastor's wife is also taking chemotherapy and radiation. It means a lot to have a friend who truly understands. The pastor and his wife often meet with Charlie and me to share and pray together." What a joy it was to hear her radiant testimony!

In mid-December, I became seriously ill and had to be off work for several months. It seemed best for me to work closer home, so I found another job.

Nearly two years later, I received a call from Jim, one of the workers from the postal hub. Around Easter 1999, I had had the blessed privilege of leading Jim and his wife to the Lord. Now he was calling to see about getting together. We had a wonderful hour of catching up on the lives of old acquaintances.

I asked, "Jim, what can you tell me about Charlie and Sue?"

"Leonard, you would not believe the change in Sue," Jim said. "She had chemotherapy and radiation. All her hair fell out; she is skin and bones. She came back to work, but she is not the same person. I don't know what happened to her, but all she can talk about is 'the Lord.' It's 'Praise the Lord' this, and 'Praise the Lord' that. You know, one of those kind; but Charlie—well, Charlie is still the same. They transferred to a less stressful facility and I've lost track of them."

Jim's visit was short, but he brought wonderful news. I was thrilled to know Sue was still living for Jesus, but my heart cries out for Charlie. *Charlie, oh Charlie, don't wait too long to make up your mind.*

Time is moving so swiftly! Oh, that I would have more opportunities to lead people to the Lord Jesus, who can change lives for all eternity.

I often ask someone I have just met, "If you were to die tonight, or even right now, do you know without a doubt that you would go to Heaven to be with Jesus?" It is a straightforward question, requiring a "Yes" or "No" answer.

How would you answer this question? You can know if you're ready to meet Jesus. Don't put it off. Talk to someone who is truly born again and proves it by living according to the Bible. They will be happy to help you. At present God's mercy is still extended to all people, but there is no promise of tomorrow.

Yes, God speaks to the world through the lives of His children. This experience has shown me in a new way how important it is to be a faithful witness.

# 14

## *He Does Hear!*

*Martha B. Shank*

Sue was overwhelmed. *How can I get everything done?* she thought. After being up much of the night with a fretful child who was teething, Sue was exhausted. Motherhood was so demanding. Sam would have helped, but he had had a hard day at work yesterday and expected another hard one today.

Now Sue's heart cried out to her Lord, "Oh, that I may know and feel Your love. I need Your help so desperately. Please, Lord!"

Feeling helpless, Sue began to fret. *I'm so tired! Why did I invite Sam's nephew and wife to stop on their way to Florida? How can I prepare a company meal? What will I cook?"*

That afternoon she opened a cabinet and was appalled at its disarray. "I really need to clean this mess while Johnny is sleeping and Darlene is happy in the sandbox. But I can't because I must make supper. But I do need to clean this kitchen, so it's ready for company. Oh, Lord, I can't get my thoughts together. I feel confused. Do You hear? Oh, what am I to do?"

Suddenly the phone rang. *Oh, no,* Sue thought, *I don't have time for another phone call.*

Sue groaned as she heard Jane's voice. Her calls were always long.

"Hello. I don't have much time to talk," said the familiar voice. "I just wanted to tell you I love you. I felt strongly led to call you this very minute. Sue, just do the *next* thing, and trust God." Sue gasped as Jane quickly added, "Goodbye for now."

Sue stood, holding the phone, staring at the receiver. "God, was that You?" she stammered. "Did Your Holy Spirit prompt Jane to call? Oh, I know it was directly from You. Thank You! You put the words I needed in her mouth. She didn't know I was overwhelmed. But You did! You used her to give me direction to 'just do the next thing!' Thank You for hearing my cry.

"Now I *will* just do the next thing—pick out a simple menu for supper. I'll use that frozen casserole I had forgotten about until just now. With canned pickles, canned fruit, and cookies left from Sunday, I'll have everything I need for supper. Yes, God, in my confusion, You have directed me with a clear plan. I praise Your name.

Darlene skipped into the kitchen for a drink of water. "God just talked to me!" Sue told her daughter. "He really does hear my prayers!"

"Mama, how did God talk to you?" the puzzled child asked.

"You see, Jane called me on the phone. You know we usually talk a long time when she calls. This time Jane just told me that she loved me, and that I should just do the next thing and trust God. I know God told her to call me. I think God put those words in her mouth. It thrills me that God did this for me."

Darlene was too young to really understand, but she caught her mother's enthusiasm. "Oh, Mama, I'm glad you are happy now."

Sue hurried to retrieve the frozen casserole from the freezer. While she was in the basement, she also chose a can of bread-and-butter pickles and a jar of peaches. "I'm glad I baked bread yesterday. Apple butter will go well with that."

She put the pickles and peaches in the refrigerator to chill. The casserole thawed on the counter.

Johnny awakened from his nap, so Sue hurried to his crib. "Oh, son, you are too little to understand, but I'll tell you anyway. God talked to me today!" To give emphasis to her joy, she held her nine-month-old close and twirled around the room. Johnny snuggled against her shoulder, relaxing as she cuddled him.

With Johnny in fresh clothes and sitting in his walker in the kitchen, Sue went about her work with renewed vigor. Little Darlene washed carefully and put on a clean dress, which her mother had selected. Next, she helped set the table, which had a clean tablecloth, carefully putting a spoon, knife, and fork at each plate. The casserole was baking in the oven. Sue's happiness pervaded the now tidy kitchen.

"I'm so excited I can hardly wait for Daddy to come home," Sue told her children. "I'll tell him how God talked to me today. And I'll tell Ron and Mabel about it too. It may strengthen their faith."

Sue took a break to call Jane. "Tell me the details, Jane. Why did you call me?"

"I was busy in the office," Jane replied, "when you suddenly came to my mind. I didn't even ponder what to say, but called you, and what I told you just rolled out. I heard you gasp, but I knew I needed to say goodbye. I did wonder how you took my call."

"Oh, Jane, I had cried out to God, 'Oh, that I can know and feel Your love.' God spoke to me through you. He *does* hear!"

# 15

## He Relieveth the Fatherless and Widow

*Julia Brubaker*

For some time I had expected that my daughter Angela would need braces. As a single mom with four children, my income as a private school teacher could not possibly pay for such a large expense. Making ends meet was a daily challenge, but the Lord met our needs in remarkable ways. Many times we were touched and humbled by the way He used other people. I will tell you of two such happenings.

When our dentist confirmed that Angela needed braces for more than cosmetic reasons, he told us it would cost 3,500 dollars.

"Well, we need to start praying for a miracle!" I said to Angela.

Angela desperately wanted the braces and began to pray fervently that God would provide the means.

A couple weeks later I took another of our children to the dentist, when out of the blue, the dentist said, "I'd like to talk with you." I followed him into another room, wondering what this could be about.

He turned to me and said, "I just wanted to tell you that I do two free orthodontic cases per year, and I would like Angela's braces to be one of them."

I was astounded! There had to be a catch! I kept asking questions until it finally sank in that the dentist really wanted to do Angela's orthodontic work—absolutely free of charge.

I said to the dentist, "Do you realize you've just answered my little girl's prayer?" The dentist had no way of knowing how low our income was; I don't think he even knew I was a single mom. He just shrugged it off, but I went home praising God for this miracle.

When I signed the papers to have the work done, the invoice read this way in the line for the charges: "Zero $ plus one cherry pie!"

You can be sure that over the years, we have happily baked many pies for the dear people in that office, and we've never forgotten how God answered Angela's prayer.

Now Angela is a lovely nineteen-year-old with a dazzling smile! We thank God.

\* \* \* \* \* \* \* \* \*

I walked out of the tire store with a heavy heart. Driving home, I pounded the steering wheel in frustration while tears streamed down my face.

My four children and I had been planning a special trip to a community six hours away. Without a husband's support and living on a church school teacher's salary, I could not afford many vacations. But I had saved up what I thought was enough for this short trip, and we were all looking forward to attending the wedding of a dear friend who had been widowed several years before.

I had come to the tire shop naively expecting a wheel alignment to straighten out whatever was making my minivan hard to steer. To my dismay I learned that I needed two new front tires and various other front-end parts to solve the problem.

After writing out a large check, I went out the door, happening to pass a well-to-do neighbor. I said a cheerful "Hello," but inside I was rebelling at the unfairness of it all.

"Why, Lord?" I cried, as I drove home. "Don't You care about us? Why do others have so much, while we struggle just to meet our basic needs?" I knew my account held enough money to cover the trip, but if we went, there would be nothing left for the utility bills that were due before my next paycheck, not to mention groceries.

By the time I reached home, I had decided we were going ahead with the trip anyway and would trust the Lord to provide for the rest of the month. I was afraid I was being irresponsible; but I kept remembering God's promises to provide for "the widow and the fatherless," and I didn't want to disappoint the children.

I must admit my faith was small as I went through the motions of pretending to enjoy the wedding. Deep inside

I was still wondering, *Does God really care about me? Does anyone know how I'm struggling? I feel so alone. I may never again know the support and care of a loving husband. I'm so tired of carrying this burden all alone.*

As I was about to leave after the wedding, a person I hardly knew came up to me and said, "When we were sitting in church, God told me I should give this to you." He pressed a wad of cash into my hand.

"Thank you," I stammered in astonishment. As we drove away, we counted up the cash. It was more than what I had spent on the van. I was so humbled and touched to realize God knew our need all along and used this special way to teach me of His love.

The children and I have been alone for almost six years now, and not once in all that time have we been unable to pay a bill on time. Over and over we have seen miracles like these. I no longer have any doubts that God is working on our behalf. Our God is mighty, and He truly does care for the fatherless and the "widow"!

# 16

## God's Blanket of Love

*Dianne Heatwole*

Thoughts of packing crowded my mind that May morning as I pulled my little car onto the road in the community where I would soon be living to head for home. If I didn't get behind a pokey driver, I could arrive home in time to have lunch with my daughter Julie and a friend who were already filling boxes at our old farmhouse. The planned moving day would dawn in a day and a half.

The miles clicked by as I drove, lost in my own thoughts. Glancing at the fuel gauge, I suddenly realized there was not enough gas to reach home. *Oh, well,* I thought, *no problem, I'll stop at the little country store at the half-way mark and fill up.*

Then another startling thought struck me. I didn't have my pocketbook! I had planned to ride home with one of my sons the night before and hadn't brought it along.

Now what? *Let's see, how much change is in the change compartment?* I carefully counted it out as I was driving. It came to one dollar and thirty-two cents. I started praying, *Lord, what should I do? One dollar and thirty-two cents won't buy a lot of gas when it sells for over two dollars a gallon.*

In the distance a white object appeared. *A kite,* I thought. Looking across the fields to see who might be flying it and watching the kite in the sky kept me preoccupied for a bit. But as I got closer, I discovered it wasn't a kite; it was a huge white bird. It dipped in front of me and flew ahead of the car for maybe a half minute before it disappeared.

A peace I cannot explain enveloped me. It seemed so clear that God was saying "All is well. I will take care of you." Singing and praising the Lord, I drove on.

The fuel gauge was mostly on empty, but going down a hill it would come up a little. I decided that when I came to the store, if the gauge was on empty, I would put in what I could with my change. If it was above empty, I would go on. As I rounded the last turn, the needle was flat on empty.

I was really hoping no one would need gas this time of day. I didn't want anyone to see me putting in my two squirts of gas. Oh, no, the little white car in front of me was pulling in also. Well, so much for privacy.

The lady driver pulled to one side of the pumps and I went to the other, purposely parking so I could turn my back and block her view. As she got out of her car, I noticed she was eyeing me carefully. I smiled to myself thinking, *I'll have my gas and be out of here long before she's done.*

Cautiously I began pumping. Two presses on the handle and I was at one dollar and thirty two cents. I sighed with relief. *Thank You, Lord, for helping me not to go over the amount of money I had.*

You can imagine my surprise when a voice said, "You need more gas than that." The lady was right at my elbow.

"Oh," I countered, "I'll be just fine."

"No," she continued, "When I pulled in, the Lord told me somebody here needed gas, and that I was to give them ten dollars. Where are you going?"

"To the Bridgewater area," I replied.

"Yes, you are the one. Now please put in ten dollars worth, and I will go pay for it." Off she went as though it were all settled.

When she returned I thanked her and offered to mail her a check, but she would have nothing to do with it. With a smile and a wave of her hand, she was gone.

The reality of what had just happened didn't sink in until I was on the road again. A wonderful feeling of being wrapped in God's blanket of love and care sent warm circles through my whole being.

Yes, with a God like *that,* we would definitely make it through the big move that loomed in front of us. Praise His Wonderful Name!

Compiler's note: This incident took place when Clair and Dianne Heatwole were in the process of answering the church's call to move to Bath County, Virginia, to help plant a new church.

# 17

# A Hard Heart
# Is Broken

*Norma Plank*
*Rewritten by permission*

I looked up as the man walked into our office. Looking into his sharp eyes, I sensed he had suffered something very traumatic. He moved warily, as if highly trained.

Behind closed doors in our conference room, he poured out his moving story. For ten years this man had worked for Kim Jong-il's directorate as an undercover agent. His mission was simple. He was to infiltrate any Christian group he could find and identify everyone involved, so they could be exterminated. But he found it was not simple; on the contrary, it was very difficult.

Most Christians remaining in North Korea have learned that, in order to survive, they must be cunning as foxes and harmless as doves. Still, this man became successful in his work against the Christians. During those ten years he found and imprisoned or executed at least

150 people. Shocked, I listened as he described an incident where he turned in a group of ten Christians. He had spent seven months watching them, their habits, their relationships, and getting to know them. Then he befriended them. After becoming accepted by a few, he showed an interest in spiritual things, and even pretended to be a Christian. He was invited to other secret meetings and slowly connected all the links. After many more months, he finally had the complete picture. In this small village in the east corner of North Korea, there were over one hundred Christians. He contacted his headquarters and troops were dispatched to collect them all.

With tearful eyes and choking with emotion, he described what followed. "There are great differences among the Christians. Some are true and some are false. When we tortured true Christians, they didn't speak, scream, argue, or curse us. They kept their thoughts to themselves. As we broke their bodies, they repeated 'Joo-Eou' (Lord) over and over like a prayer."

A sob wracked his frame, and then he continued his confession. "No matter what torture we applied: the positions, the water, the hot irons, pincers, the plastic bags, the cutting, the violations . . . they would not break. They would not deny their Lord. Not even in death." He paused.

Hot tears streamed from my eyes as I waited for him to compose himself. His expression changed as he continued, "But the others, the ones who lacked a strong faith, were screaming before we touched them. They quickly denied Christ and swore to follow Kim Jong-il. They suffered and died badly, having given up their faith. They gained nothing; they lost it all."

I looked with amazement on the man sitting stiffly before me, a persecutor of the church, a torturer and murderer. Mixed feelings coursed through me. Here sat a secret police officer describing how brutally North Korea deals with our fellow believers. Here was a man confessing great sin. Here was a fellow Christian—a man like Saul.

After a time, I asked how he became a Christian.

"Near the end of 1998 I got careless, and the government security agents somehow caught up with me," he replied. "They jailed me, as if I were just another Christian, with the political prisoners. They beat me and tortured me. I, as an undercover agent, had been taught this iron-like rule: 'Never disclose your identity, under any circumstances, to anyone, ever.' The torture intensified. I was near death when something weakened within me. I thought, *I will not die for Kim Jong-il. I want to die like those true Christians did.*

"Knowing I was signing my own death warrant, I disclosed the fact that I was a Christian. I was beaten even more and thrown out. Cursing, the officer ordered me to report to headquarters at once. I knew I would be instantly executed. Instead of obeying his orders, I quickly made my way home, picked up my two sons, and ran for the border.

"The guards saw my two sons and me rushing to cross the frozen river. The night exploded with staccato machine-gun bursts. Bullets slammed into the ice around

us, cracking it open to reveal the dark water beneath.
Pushing my terrified sons in ahead of me, I dove under-
water. Crashing through the ice, I cried out to God,
'Hananim, forgive me! Protect me!'

"With the pain of the freezing water, I remembered the
composed faces of the Christians I had slowly killed. Suddenly it was as if I entered another world. Peace came over
me. I was comforted. Somehow both my children and I
made it across the river. We ran through the rice paddy
but the sharp, cut-off stems did not hurt us. A squad of
eight Chinese border patrols jumped off their truck when
they heard the shooting and began searching all around
us. After thirty minutes they gave up and left. We ran
without direction until we couldn't run anymore. Freezing
and exhausted, I decided to just go to the nearest house
and give the children up."

He stopped his story for a moment and reached for
some more tea, as if to warm himself, and then continued. "When I knocked on the door, a light came on. The
door opened and people with beautiful, glowing faces
invited us in. They clothed us, fed us, and spoke to us
about Jesus. Somehow, without any way of knowing
which direction to run, we had made our way directly to
a Korean-Chinese church.

"A few days later, after getting to know the pastor and
his family, I confessed my shameful past. We cried
together. He showed me from the Bible how I could
receive God's forgiveness, and how I could give my loyalty
to Jesus Christ. I am so unworthy . . ."

# III.

## GOD SPEAKS THROUGH

*Circumstances*

# 18

## A Battle With Polio

*Waneta Sandlin*
*As told to Norma Plank*

In my twenties I worked for several years in Newfound, Kentucky, as a missionary-helper with Ezra and Vida Good and their family of five children. I enjoyed working in their home, giving Bible lessons in one-room schools, teaching Sunday school classes at church, teaching summer Bible school, and visiting homes. We rejoiced when people decided to follow the Lord.

Newfound was a rough country; our travel was by horse, mule, or jeep—and of course by walking. The roads were hilly, very narrow, and rough with rocks and muddy ruts. At times a creek bed served as a road. In Newfound, the Lord taught me an important lesson through a very hard experience.

In the summer of 1952, a couple of friends from our home church at Elida, Ohio, came to visit me. On a Sunday evening we went to Gays Creek, Kentucky, some fifty miles away, to hear a program by young folks from

Pennsylvania. I didn't feel well, and wondered if I was starting the flu. I had a sore throat, fever, and headache, and my legs ached terribly. Rather than traveling the rough roads back to Newfound in the dark, we spent the night with my cousin, Mrs. Marion Hartman, who lived at Wild Cat, Kentucky.

On Monday morning my friends returned to Elida, and Marion drove me back to the North Fork River, which was about three miles from Ezra's. I crossed the long swinging bridge spanning the river and walked to Ezra's, but I could feel the muscles in my right leg drawing up. I was miserable. My misery continued. Some days I would feel a bit better, but then I'd take a turn for the worse.

Vida's father, B. B. King, came to hold a week of revival meetings, which I had been eagerly looking forward to. Brother King was a special person in my life, because twelve years earlier he had baptized me. I hadn't seen him for ten or more years.

Though I didn't feel like it, I went along to church Sunday, and following the service, ate dinner in one of the local homes.

On Monday my legs and head hurt terribly, but I forced myself to help with the washing because there was a lot to do. When Ezra's and Brother King went visiting in homes in the community, I was told to rest, which I tried to do. On Wednesday I thought I was slightly improved, but my right leg was weak and sometimes gave way so that I nearly fell. My temperature was almost normal.

My uncle and aunt, Merlin and Esther Good, had invited us all out to Wild Cat for dinner. I didn't feel up to it, so I stayed home to finish the ironing. Just as they were leaving, Vida came back in and took my temperature. It was up again.

"You're going to the doctor," she said.

The doctor wasn't very concerned.

"Could it be polio?" Vida asked.

"You missionaries think of the worst things," the doctor replied. He gave me a prescription and said, "Come back in a day or two if you're not better."

From the doctor we went to my uncle's house, and I lay down to rest a while. When I got up, my neck was stiff. I spent the night at my uncle's place. Aunt Esther gave me a pain pill, which helped me sleep, but in the morning my leg was no better. They decided to take me to another doctor.

"She has polio," he said right away.

I cried, imagining myself an invalid for the rest of my life. The future looked very dark. When the doctor realized my family lived at Elida and that I wanted to go home, he said, "If you leave right away, you may travel to Ohio, but you must get to the hospital as soon as possible."

It was a difficult eight-hour trip. While lying in the back seat of my cousin's car, a battle raged in my heart. *Why? Why? Why, Lord? Why would You take me from the mission field, where I was trying to serve You faithfully? Why would You force me into seclusion in the hospital, when I long to tell others about You? Then likely I'll be a cripple all my life. I need Your help, Lord. I don't want to end up bitter and useless. It's hard, Lord, but yes, I want You to mold me and make me after Your own will.*

When I submitted my will to the Father's, I felt His comforting arms about me and peace began to flood my soul.

On August 1, 1952, I started a three-week stay in the Lima Memorial Hospital. I was only in isolation for one day, because it had been nearly three weeks since I started the disease and the contagious period was already passed.

I soon learned that the Lord had not shuttled me into seclusion when he sent me to the hospital. My cousin's wife came to the hospital nearly every day to see her baby son, who was very sick. She was not a Christian, and we really didn't know one another very well, but she always stopped in to see me. She was truly seeking God and was full of questions about the Christian life. During my three-week stay, I had several different roommates. They and the nurses asked many questions about God. I could almost hear the Lord gently speaking, *Waneta, do you understand why I brought you here for such a time as this?*

*Yes, Lord, I understand. Please forgive me for asking why!*

After leaving the hospital, I continued to receive therapy to strengthen my right leg. Many people prayed for me, and God allowed me to come through with only a limp.

Eight months later, I returned to the mission field—with some limitations, but able to help. I praise God for His goodness to me.

# 19

## He Made My Nose

*Norma Plank*

Did you ever wish your blue eyes were black or your brown eyes were green? Did you ever long for shiny black hair instead of blond? I did. Maybe you wish you hadn't been born with a crippled leg or poor eyesight or with a lisp in your speech. Most of us have sometime or other wished God had made us a bit differently.

When I was twelve years old, I looked in the mirror and made a shocking discovery! I learned that my nose was big—too big, too long—and the nostrils were embarrassingly large. Why me, Lord? Some of my friends had cute little noses. Why couldn't I have a pretty nose? Whose fault was it? We always like to blame someone else for our problems.

My mother always reminded us children, "Don't *schnupps* (sniffle)! Blow your nose!" Did my nose stretch from too much blowing?

Hardly!

Then I remembered that children often look somewhat like their parents. My parents didn't know it, but I thoroughly investigated their noses—from the side, from the front, from below. I had never noticed before, but sure enough, they both had large noses, very similar in shape. Why, oh, why, did this tragedy have to happen to me? It was their fault. Then it occurred to me: maybe they didn't like their nose shape and size any more than I did. They had had no opportunity to order a perfect nose either.

Why did my parents have big noses? This is what I discovered. My father's parents both had large, humpy noses. Next, I looked at my mother's parents. Grandma's nose was rather cute. But Grandpa—well, he had the largest of them all, and to top it off, it had lots of ugly red veins. It was clear that my parents hadn't had a chance to have a nice nose. I'm sorry to say I grew up through my teen years feeling inferior, and I blushed easily.

A likable young fellow in our youth group enjoyed teasing me. "Hey, look at her blush," he would say. By then, I wasn't just blushing; I was crimson. I was sure my friends were noticing my nose. I laughed it off, but it was embarrassing. I spent too much time checking other people's noses and wondering, *Why, why, why couldn't my nose be like theirs?*

One day I read something in my Bible, and I felt as if my kind heavenly Father had given me a spanking. I deserved it, and I think He had reason to be tired of my attitude about the way He had made me. Here is the verse: "Nay but, O man, who art thou that repliest against

God? Shall the thing formed say to him that formed it, Why hast thou made me thus?" (Romans 9:20).

I was guilty, and I knew it. I had been unhappy with the way God made me. I told the Lord I was sorry for complaining, but I still couldn't say, "Thank You, Lord, for making me like this."

One day I found another verse: "But now, O LORD, thou art our father; we are the clay, and thou our potter; and we all are the work of thy hand" (Isaiah 64:8).

I pondered that verse. Did God really mean we *all* were the work of His hand? What about the crippled, the blind, and the deaf and dumb?

Later, I found this verse: "And the LORD said unto him, Who hath made man's mouth? or who maketh the dumb, or deaf, or the seeing, or the blind? Have not I the LORD?" (Exodus 4:11). I was convinced that God knew what He was doing when He made me.

Years later, the Lord showed me a sight that revolutionized my thinking about my nose. I was in the checkout line in a drugstore when a woman in front of me turned around to talk to a tiny man, who was a midget. I'm sure my eyes bulged and my jaw dropped a couple inches. She had no nose! There were two holes in her face where her nose should have been. A short piece of skin like a fish worm dangled between her eyes. As soon as I got over the shock of it, I found my heart crying out to God, "Oh Lord, please forgive me for ever complaining about my nose. Thank You, O Lord, thank You, for my nose—just the way You made it."

I began counting my blessings. Why, I had a perfectly good nose! I could smell nice things—a peace rose, gingerbread fresh from the oven, newly-mown hay, lilacs, and lilies of the valley. I could wrinkle up my nose when something smelled bad. I could breathe the nice cool morning air. I was even grateful for the little hairs that grew inside my nose to protect my lungs from the dust and for my super drainpipe—when I caught a cold.

The lady with no nose never realized it, but because of her, honor, praise, and thanksgiving ascended from me to my Creator. Also, I had admired that lady and midget man for accepting themselves the way God made them and to humbly go about everyday life. They could have become bitter and refused to step outside their house— but they didn't. I'm sure we can all think of people who have been a wonderful blessing to us because of their handicap and the courageous way they faced life. The Lord used His Word and this woman to speak to my heart and to whittle me down to where He wanted me.

No, God was not asleep while you and I were being made. No other person in the whole world is exactly like you or me. Therefore no one can perform our job in the way He planned for us to do it. It is exciting to know that God has a wonderful plan for each of our lives, and the way He formed us will help us fulfill that plan.

# "Mommy, What's Heaven Like?"

*Chester Heatwole*

In the Peake community lived a sweet six-year-old girl. One day she began asking her nonChristian mother many unusual and strange questions about Heaven.

Her mother was very surprised and wondered why such a young girl would ask such questions. But God has some very unusual ways of speaking to mothers and to communities. Sometimes He even uses little girls.

The next day, this little girl was run over by a dump truck and killed. Her questions about Heaven and her death spoke loudly to her mother and the whole community. Everyone was deeply touched; their minds were drawn heavenward.

Many times God allows unusual things to happen in families, in communities, and in the world to get the sinner's, as well as the saint's, attention.

# 21

## And I Sat Where They Sat

*Norma Plank*

*For our light affliction, which is but for a moment, worketh
for us a far more exceeding and eternal weight of glory.*
2 Corinthians 4:17

Have you ever thought about how our suffering helps
us to better understand others who are suffering? No
wonder our Lord instructs us to give thanks for all things.
He wants His children to be well equipped to help suffering humanity, so they can see the likeness of Christ in us.

I once experienced suffering, for which I truly thank
God. It was a real eye-opener.

For two and a half years, Don and I were caretakers
and business manager for a large campground in Georgia.
Many Christian families and church groups rented the
facilities throughout the year.

On July 16, 1999, we were hurriedly mowing the huge lawn—Don on the farm tractor with a pull-along mower in the front lawn, and I on the riding lawn mower behind the fellowship hall. We wanted the Center to look nice for a large group that was coming to rent the facility. I had the mower in high gear because the grass wasn't thick, but there was an abundance of those tall spiky weeds with yellow flowers, which gave the lawn a shaggy, untidy look. When Don purchased the used mower, we weren't aware the brakes were bad, but we had learned to gear it down when heading down a hill and had gotten along quite well up to this point.

Suddenly I realized I was going down a gentle slope, and I had failed to shift into a lower gear. *Uh-oh,* I thought, *Don told me to gear this thing down on a hill.* I shoved in the clutch, hoping to do just that, but the hill was steeper now and that mower took off like a scared rabbit, bouncing over terrain never intended for mowing and heading straight for the lake. It's a miracle the mower was not ruined.

I was thrown from the mower and knocked unconscious. When I landed, the skin was scraped off my left kneecap, and dirt and grit were embedded into the raw flesh. As soon as I left the seat, the motor and cutting blades stopped, but the mower wheel ran over the backside of my left leg, badly bruising my calf.

When I came to, I saw the mower had stopped before it went into the lake. What a relief! I tried repeatedly to get to my feet, only to fall back down. I knew it could be an hour before Don would come looking for me. Then I remembered the many hills of vicious fire ants. *What if I'm lying on an anthill? I wondered.* That thought motivated me greatly. I gritted my teeth and scrambled to my feet, feeling sure that bones were broken in my shoulders and ribs. I started hobbling toward our house.

When I got within sight of Don, he hollered, "Did you run out of gas?"

"No, I'm hurt," I said, clutching my left arm against my chest.

He was soon at my side, helping me to the house. Together, we cleaned the dirt and grit from my raw kneecap, poured on peroxide and vitamin E and applied a bandage. We then called for Stan O'Bannon, who is an EMT. After a brief examination, he encouraged us to go to the hospital and have some x-rays done, which we did. My collarbone and shoulder blade were both broken—plus some ribs. Oh, the misery!

Suddenly, I was becoming familiar with a new experience. Although I was nearly seventy years of age, I had never known how helpless the elderly feel in the many care centers where I have sung and visited. But now I needed Don's help just to get off my chair so I could stand to my feet, to lie down, to get up in the morning, to get dressed, and to bathe. And to top it off, I couldn't comb my hair. Don had his first experience in braiding hair! To say the least, I looked awful. I was thankful that my head veiling covered most of the mess. Don did his best, and I was very thankful for his help.

I remember one evening vividly. I was sitting on the edge of the bed, dreading the painful ordeal of being helped to lie down for the night. Tears were rolling down my cheeks. I knew I was being a big baby, but I couldn't prepare my mind to face the pain. After waiting patiently for a while (at least outwardly), Don suddenly had me lying down before I realized what happened. I was thankful he made the decision for me, for then I could sigh contentedly while the pain subsided.

The girls' and boys' camps were in session while I recuperated. One day a group of girls and their leader kindly came and sang for me. They didn't know it, but God was teaching me through them what it was like to be sung to instead of being one of the singers, and also how it felt to be caught among my pillows in a recliner and with my hair a mess.

*Thank You, Lord,* I prayed silently, *for teaching me through this painful experience. Now I know what it's like for those dear souls in the many care centers. I didn't know they felt this helpless and ugly. Oh, Lord, may I have greater compassion for those dear ones, who don't have the hope of healing and better days ahead, which I have. I truly am thankful for this valuable lesson, dear Lord.*

I don't want to end this article on such a note—making the elderly feel like having a "pity party." There is also a bright side to my experience, and no doubt they've had similar experiences. My step-granddaughter, Beth Plank, came and helped me for one week; singers came; people brought in food ready to eat; flowers arrived; the board members for the camp ground purchased a nice, new mower (with brakes); cards and letters came in abundance; visitors came; there were phone calls, faxes, and e-mails. My stepson, Dave Plank, who is a physician's assistant, gave us some medical advice. It's so nice to know that when we get old and helpless, there will always be those who so willingly give the help needed.

I thank God for the many experiences He allows His children to go through, so we can better serve Him, and that He showers us all with many blessings whether we are the helpless one or the helper. God is so good!

# 22

## Hidden Tracts

*Becky McGurrin*

*Oh, I'd better hide these before Joe sees them,* thought Becky as she scooped up the pile of tracts. *I wonder how they got here in the dining room. I don't remember reading them recently.*

She had felt drawn to those tracts ever since she had first spotted them on the table at the homeschooling convention a few months ago. They were so interesting—compelling, you might say; and their message, though new to her, had found a comfortable place in her heart.

Both Becky and Joe had been raised in the Roman Catholic faith, so they were familiar with the Bible and the stories it contained. What's more, the last five years they had attended an interdenominational Bible church, which had stirred in them a desire to know Jesus more intimately and to walk more closely with Him in all areas of their lives.

But Becky and Joe secretly became more and more dissatisfied with what they saw. Though the church professed to follow the Bible, it ignored Bible teachings on many subjects. Topics such as returning good for evil, modesty in appearance, and living in nonconformity to the world were either ignored or scoffed at by many church members. Why did the Bible teach a holy way of life while the church promoted the very opposite?

But these tracts were different. They actually encouraged Christians to literally follow the teachings of the New Testament. "We are supposed to follow in Jesus' footsteps," they taught, "and do everything in a way that would please Him."

It thrilled Becky's heart to know there really were people out there somewhere who hungered and thirsted after righteousness the way she did. That is why she had spent so many hours reading and rereading the tracts and imagining how pleasant it would be to live among and fellowship with such people.

*I wonder what these people are like,* she pondered as she fingered the tracts once again. *Who are they and where do they live?* As anxious as she was to meet the people who had written the tracts, she was reluctant to share these thoughts with her dear husband. She feared that he would be disturbed by her dissatisfaction with their current church life and become worried that she was becoming some kind of fanatic. So she hurried to hide her secret before Joe got home from work.

*Lord,* she prayed as she carried the precious booklets up to their bedroom. *I'm so confused. Here I am hiding good things from my husband. This can't be right. What should I do? The teaching of these tracts seems so Biblical—so right.*

*But who am I to disagree with my whole church? Am I wiser than my pastors? Oh, Father, forgive me for questioning. I just want to know the way You want me to go. Please show Your will very clearly so that I can follow You. Help me to know how to walk in truth.*

As she opened the drawer to put away her treasure, Becky was met with an unbelievable sight. Though she held a full set of tracts in her hand, an identical set of tracts was already lying in the drawer!

*How can there be two identical sets of tracts when I only picked up one set at the convention?* she wondered as she heard Joe pull into the driveway. *That's it,* she thought, *these tracts must belong to Joe! Lord, could it be? Are You speaking to both of us at the same time?*

She rushed back down the stairs with both sets of tracts and met her husband at the door. Before he had a chance to say hello, she blurted out, "Are these yours?"

With a startled and somewhat sheepish look, Joe nodded. "Did I forget to put them away this morning?" he asked. "I was hoping you wouldn't find them yet. I picked them up at the last homeschooling convention, and I've been reading them a lot. They have some interesting things to say."

"I know they do," said Becky with a smile as she held up her own set of booklets. "They say the same thing my tracts do."

After the children had been put to bed, Joe and Becky sat down for a long-dreaded, but now much desired, conversation.

"I've really felt drawn to these tracts," he began. "They agree so clearly with the Bible that they are hard to ignore. I've been so afraid to tell you because I know how much you love our church, but I think God is soon going to move us into the next chapter of our lives. Do you think you're ready?"

"Oh, Joe," she replied, "I'm not happy at church any more. I've been dissatisfied ever since I first realized we were being hindered from walking more closely with Jesus. I didn't tell you because I didn't want to upset you."

"And to think, here God was speaking plainly to both of us, but we were afraid to tell each other. I feel like a fool!"

"Well, that's two of us then," she agreed with a chuckle. "What do we do now?"

"I don't see that we have much choice, do we?" responded Joe. "We'll try to contact these people and learn more about them. It says here on the bottom of this tract that they're called Mennonites."

And so began our search for the separated ones, the peculiar people, the Anabaptists. It wasn't long before we found and joined the Mennonite people in Virginia and West Virginia. We cheerfully began to live the type of holy life that was first described to us by some *hidden* tracts.

# Disappointment—
# His Appointment

*Julia Brubaker*

*Oh no, Lord! How can this be happening to me,* I cried inwardly. *Here I am at an airport—two-and-a-half hours from home—and my flight is cancelled.*

I had planned my trip so carefully and with such happy anticipation! It would be the first time in some twenty years that I was flying alone, all the way from my home in Alberta to Pennsylvania, for a broken homes seminar at Penn Valley.

"No problem," the ticket agent said. "We'll just reroute you at our expense. You can take the next flight east, which leaves at two o'clock this afternoon, and overnight in Minneapolis. Your room will be paid for by the airline, of course."

No problem? Well, it looked simple to them, but that option was rather intimidating to a thirty-nine-year-old

Mennonite lady. I had recently been separated from my husband of seventeen years, and I was not at all used to traveling alone. The idea of a night alone in a large city was frightening. Besides, my aunt and uncle had planned to pick me up that evening in Harrisburg, and I didn't know if it would suit them to wait till the next day. Nothing was working out according to my carefully laid plans.

I tried to think if I knew anyone close to Minneapolis with whom I might spend the night. I started making phone calls, but wasn't really getting anywhere, when into the airport walked some relatives. Their daughter was booked on the same cancelled flight to a teacher's convention in Pennsylvania. So they were looking for other options too. Their daughter Martha decided to fly to Baltimore and spend the night with some friends near Lancaster. After contacting my aunt and uncle, I decided to go with her to Baltimore.

It was a long and taxing day, but, to my relief, I didn't have to fly alone after all. And Martha's friends made us welcome and gave us a bed for the night when we staggered in close to midnight.

I was having a hard time seeing why things had to work out this way, but I kept remembering Romans 8:28: "All things work together for good to them that love God," and wondering if I would ever know what God's purpose was in this change of plans.

After a rather sleepless night in a hot upstairs bedroom (I wasn't used to the oppressive Pennsylvania heat!) I went downstairs for breakfast, a little shy about imposing on these strangers.

Then the phone rang, and to my surprise, it was for me. The caller was a dear friend whom I had known since our teens. We had become especially close while we were both going through some rough waters. However, we hadn't any contact for the last couple of years and I didn't even know where she lived. It turned out that she was now living in the very community in which I had spent the night. Somehow she found out I was there and wanted to see me again. She took me to a restaurant where we had several very special hours of sharing.

Later, my aunt and uncle picked me up and took me to Penn Valley in good time for the seminar.

I rejoiced as I realized that, once again, God had everything under control. If my flight had not been cancelled, I would never have had that wonderful visit with Alice. God knew ahead of time what would happen. He worked my disappointment out for His glory and my good. So now, when things don't seem to be working out the way I want, I start wondering what other plan God might have in store. When I commit my circumstances to Him, amazing things can happen. Yes, God can speak to me and reveal His plan through circumstances.

# 24

## God Still Loves Me!

*Carolyn Roth*

"God, where are You? Why have You turned Your face from me? Why don't You answer my prayers?" Sandy cried out to the Lord for the umpteenth time.

Life looked overwhelming. Stresses mounted. Unusual challenges at church and the school demanded more than normal job hours from her pastor-husband; her mother-in-law was dying from liver cancer; their tiny baby came down with a severe cold; and two preschoolers needed her as well. Never had she experienced such darkness of soul. Never had she felt so much in need of God's strength and love. Sandy's usual cheery optimism had fled before the winter storms.

Thursday was the day for her postpartum checkup, so she bundled little Benjamin into snowsuit and blankets. It would take an hour through city traffic to reach the hospital. She needed the check-up, and she wanted the midwives to meet six-week-old Benjamin. In the waiting room Sandy tried to calm her anxieties and to cast her worries on the Lord.

"Do you have an appointment today?" queried the receptionist.

"Yes, I'm here to see my midwife for my six-week checkup," Sandy clarified.

Scanning the roster, the receptionist shook her head. "You won't believe this, but your appointment is tomorrow. Your midwifery team is not even in today."

*It was the last straw!*

Temperatures in the single digits had reduced their patient load that day, so they offered Sandy a slot with a different team of midwives.

Sandy accepted their offer. While she continued waiting, she poured out her heart to the Lord again.

Suddenly, the door to the waiting room opened and a voice exclaimed, "Sandy!"

Sandy could not believe her eyes. There stood her midwife! When Sandy explained why she was there, her midwife arranged to attend to her personally.

Light broke through Sandy's stress clouds in that moment. In the depths of her innermost being Sandy heard, "God loves me!"

That perfect timing was orchestrated by a Sovereign and loving heavenly Father. That little act of kindness was a powerful, concrete, and miraculous intervention from the Father of Light! God spoke His love to a weary soul.

# 25

## A Bit Crowded

*Willy Waldner*

Our single-wide mobile home was crowded, and my wife and I began praying about a larger house for our growing family. We had six children and were expecting another in the spring. In addition, we wanted to be able sometimes to keep overnight guests.

So we prayed about what we should do. "Should we build on a room or two or look for a bigger house?" we asked the Lord.

One day my dad told me that the Hutterites in a nearby farming community were getting rid of their old houses and building new ones. My mind was racing. *Is God providing a way for us?* After I left, I didn't wait to get home but quickly phoned about the houses. The person in charge said all their houses had been sold to a moving company. There were five large houses—enough to house about twenty-five families. I immediately phoned the moving company and asked what they were doing with those houses.

I was thrilled when I heard, "They're for sale."

One house interested me more than the rest, but other people wanted it too, he explained. But he set up an appointment to see if I could buy it. About a week later, a contact man came to our farm to make the deal. I could hardly believe my ears. Yes, when he left, we were the future owners of the house we wanted.

We did have to wait. Before they could move the house, the Hutterites had to first build new houses. But in less than one year after making the deal, our house was moved onto a newly prepared basement on our farm. When the house was lowered onto the basement walls, it fit so well that there was no more than a 1½ inch variation anywhere.

Deep thankfulness welled up in my heart. "Praise the Lord," I said.

The original house was 125 x 40 feet, which was more than we needed. So we sold 50 x 40 feet to another buyer, and we still have a good-sized house. Four months to the day after it was moved onto our farm, we moved into the freshly painted house with new flooring and a new kitchen. We are so thankful for God's great blessings to us.

Considering how many people were interested in the house, we count it a direct leading of the Lord to allow us to use it during our short pilgrimage on earth. We're looking forward to the day when we can move to a new home whose builder and maker is God.

# 26

## Great Is Thy Faithfulness

*Dora Waldner*

The day began just like any other day on the farm. We got up, dressed the children, prepared and ate breakfast, and had family devotions.

My husband Willie and our son David were going to a farm-machinery auction. Nine-year-old Willie Jr. was instructed to do the chores.

I was busy baking and working in the house with the rest of the children. It was not unusual for Willie Jr. to ask if Debbie and Johnny could go with him. The little ones could enjoy the animals while he did the chores. I agreed.

They weren't gone long before Willie Jr. came walking home with Johnny and two-year-old Debbie. Willie Jr. looked worried and shaken. By nature he is calm and quiet, but now he was talking nonstop. I couldn't follow what was disturbing him.

"Mom, you must come to the shop and see what Debbie did."

I quickly got my shoes and coat and hurried to the shop with the two children beside me. They were both talking at once, trying to explain what had happened. When we got to the shop, I could hardly believe what I saw.

Part of our shop was rented out to some people who made greenhouses to sell. The rented part was partitioned off with clear, heavy plastic curtains hung from steel cables. All their supplies were laid out on tables and carts.

Two weeks earlier we had bought a four-wheeler for Willie Jr.'s ninth birthday. Really, it was more of a farm tool, but it was presented on the day of his birthday.

Now surveying the scene, I reconstructed what had happened. When the children arrived at the shop, they saw the four-wheeler. Debbie and Johnny begged Willie Jr. to start it up and give them a ride around the shop, which they knew was strictly forbidden.

The temptation was strong, and Willie Jr. gave in. He let Debbie go first, allowing her to sit in front of him and steer. They didn't go far till Willie Jr. realized he couldn't reach the controls from where he was sitting. He could neither stop it nor turn it around! Debbie backed up and turned at the same time, and the four-wheeler got tangled in the plastic curtain dividing the shop. Willie Jr. screamed at Debbie to stop, but little Debbie only kept on and backed that four-wheeler up onto the work tables packed and stacked with all kinds of things for building greenhouses. The four-wheeler, which weighs over one thousand pounds, was almost standing on its nose and would have fallen forward and crushed the two children, except that the cable which held up the curtain had wound itself around the back wheels.

God used the cable to hang up that four-wheeler and hold it while our children got off safely and came to me for help.

When I saw all of this, I remember saying aloud, "Great is Thy faithfulness!" It could have been so different had not the angels watched over our children that day.

When Daddy got home and cut the cable, the four-wheeler fell, damaging it enough that it needed repairs. Quite a bit of damage had been done to the tables and supplies too.

The Lord spoke loudly to me that day and showed me "He is God," and it was He who spared our children. I was moved to tears. He alone controls what happens in the lives of his children. Nine months earlier, we had lost our 3½-month-old baby and our family was still grieving, so we were doubly thankful for God's protecting hand that day. I want to continue telling people of His greatness and goodness to our family.

# God's Almighty Hand

*Norma Plank*

When Hurricane Katrina roared ashore in August 2005, the coastal areas of Mississippi and Louisiana suffered tremendous damage. Stories of widespread destruction, human suffering, and needs filled the news. During this time my husband Don and I visited a dear friend, Jim Burke, a Jewish believer.

While we were visiting, Jim told us an exciting story about his brother Vincent, who lives in Mississippi near the Gulf of Mexico. When his brother heard that Hurricane Katrina was about to make landfall, he walked the perimeter of his property, praying that God would place his angels to stand guard and protect his property, his family, and himself. When he went back inside, he continued to pray throughout the storm.

When the storm was over, he opened his door and stepped outside to survey the damage. Other than a few shingles torn from his roof and a large refrigerator parked on his front lawn, his house was in fine shape. But all around his property there was destruction. The waters of the Gulf had come crashing in to within three houses of his home.

Astonished people started coming and asking, "Why is your house standing undamaged, and our houses are in shambles?"

It was evident God wanted to use this miracle to speak to these people. Vincent was happy for the privilege to witness for his Lord. He quickly told them it was the Lord's doing, how he had walked around his property and prayed, asking for God's protection.

The result of that testimony was that many people were led to the Saviour.

Vincent's next prayer was, "Lord, send pastors to guide these people. They are sheep without a shepherd."

We have since learned that there are pastors rising to the challenge to give these dear souls spiritual guidance.

We serve a great God; He is almighty!

# 28

## *Our Sofa Speaks*

*Ellen (Barnhart) Heatwole*

"No, no, no! It can't be! But it is—another bill from the hospital." That was my reaction one February day as I opened the mailbox. I had hoped to receive something that might lift my drooping spirits. Instead, here was a bill from the hospital reminding us, not so gently, that our bill hadn't been paid in full.

Just the month before, Elam had arranged with the personnel office to pay one hundred dollars per month. They agreed and we had been meeting that quota. However, the computer hadn't heard that agreement and did what it was programmed to do—send one bill, followed by another, and then add some choice punches.

I knew Elam would call the office to make sure they were aware of his agreement. "They wrote it down," he assured me, "but probably the computer failed to get that message."

I thanked God for Elam's sincere integrity and skillful handling of our financial affairs, complicated though they seemed at times. I had confidence he would handle this one just as wisely, but still, I couldn't shake that awful sense of despair.

*Why do we have to receive letters like this when we always try to meet our obligations? What is God trying to teach us in these devastating experiences? Are we destined to go through life with our hopes and dreams shattered again and again? Are we so stupid we can't learn what God is trying to teach us, so the exams must be repeated over and over in the school of hard knocks?*

And then a gentle voice admonished, "It's time to hear the sofa speak its message again."

So I plopped down on the sofa and whispered, "Speak, sofa, speak. I need your message ever so badly." A tear trickled down my cheek.

Linden, just turned five, came in and crawled up beside me. "Mother, why is your face like that?" he questioned innocently, spying my tears.

"Do you remember how we got this sofa, Linden?"

"Yes, Mother, I remember. God sent it last year."

"Linden, I just needed to come in and think about how God gave us this sofa and be reminded that He will always take care of us."

"Well, why does that make your face like that?"

How do you explain the emotions that arise from remembering the six-year battle against a genetic disease resulting in his sister's death only seven months ago or the disappointment of receiving a bill from his hospitalization that was triggered by the very same disease? How do you build faith in an innocent, ever-so-precious five-year-old—when your own faith so badly needs bolstering?

"See this, Linden?" I tried to explain, "It's a bill from the hospital. It just makes me sad to think about when you were so sick in the hospital and to remember how sick Jewel was last year. That's why my face is like that. But let's think about this sofa and how God gave it to us."

"Tell me, Mother. Tell me again about the sofa," begged Linden.

\* \* \* \* \* \* \* \* \*

The story of our sofa is very precious indeed, a reminder of God's constant care in our lives. And when I need a boost, like I do this morning, it always helps to stop and let that sofa speak.

Eleven months ago the telephone rang and a cheery voice wondered, "Will you be home Tuesday?"

"Sure. Why?"

"A furniture store will be delivering a hide-a-bed sofa sometime next Tuesday."

"Well . . . how and why?"

"We received a refund from our income tax," the voice said, "and we used that to buy a sofa for you. We knew you really needed it, but we knew if we gave you the money you'd use it to pay doctor bills. So we've picked out a sofa and it will be delivered Tuesday."

Tears of humble gratitude muffled my heart-felt thanks and set my mind to rolling. *So this is how God was answering our prayer from nine months ago.*

Before the birth of our third child, we debated and prayed about what to do. The old sofa was stained and tattered from hosting sick children. It had been vomited on and spit-up on and endured bladder accidents as well. I had shampooed and scrubbed it repeatedly. Though sanitized, it refused to look nice. A new sofa was out of the question. When a friend suggested towels for a cover, we felt content. Our need met, we quit praying about the sofa and now, nine months later, God sent a brand-new one through our door. What a mighty God we serve! Who else gives the desires of our heart?

Never will I forget that evening as we all sat on God's gift to us while having our family devotions. Jewel and Linden were so excited about the new sofa from God. Crystal, at nine months, too little to know what the excitement meant, joined in nevertheless. And then Elam thanked God for the sofa and prayed we would always use it for His glory.

That sofa episode was a mountaintop experience. God knew we needed it. In a few weeks Jewel got much worse and was transferred from our local hospital to the university hospital sixty miles away. Those were two difficult weeks, trying to meet the needs of a terminally ill child, a ten-month-old nursing baby, and a four-year-old toddler.

Family and church friends helped us through. The sofa's message was reassuring during that time and in the trying months that followed as Jewel's disease progressed.

During the days after Jewel's death in July, around one hundred people came to see us and sat on God's sofa.

God knew much better than we when we would need that piece of furniture. Through that experience we learned God doesn't grant us all the desires of our hearts, only the ones that coincide with His perfect will and timing. In spite of death and its trauma, our sofa spoke a powerful sermon of God's kind, loving care.

In December, we hosted overnight friends. Young Daniel and his brother slept on our sofa—converted into a bed. I heard him whisper, "This is the best bed in the world."

According to bed ratings, it really wasn't; he was just tired. But I wholeheartedly agreed. For us, it was the best bed in the world because it came from the very heart and hand of God.

That night our sofa spoke of hope. Maybe our being able to host overnight guests spoke of our ability to be hospitable and normal again. That night as Elam and I retired on the floor, our hearts felt happy, truly happy. Our heaven-sent sofa had opened the door of hope.

And then three weeks later, Linden was in the hospital, a very sick little boy. We had been so thankful because he had been so well. We had even dared to hope the Lord would heal him. But now hope fled. Only six months ago his six-year-old sister had died, leaving a terrible void in our family circle. Fear engulfed us. Would we be called to repeat that experience?

How we rejoiced when Linden responded to treatment and was able to return home again. Then complications set in, and he lay listless on the sofa, his face contorted with pain. (And I didn't need to ask him, "Why is your face like that?") Gradually he improved, but something had happened to our spirit of euphoria and the hope we had experienced the night young Daniel slept on our "sofa that speaks."

Then our chimney caught fire, causing minor wall damage in several rooms. Linden, not quite fully recovered, experienced fear upon fear. He literally shook— fearing our house would burn. Several fire trucks sitting in our driveway and firemen everywhere failed to excite his boyish ambitions. Even the fire chief, taking time to sit down beside him and reassure him by telling him he wouldn't let our house burn, didn't calm him. Who could blame him? In six short months he had undergone three traumatic experiences—the death of his older sister, his first hospitalization, and fear of all fears—a fire.

We pleaded for wisdom from our heavenly Father—the God who gives sofas—to know how to meet the needs and calm the fears of this precious child. We found our God to be able.

\* \* \* \* \* \* \* \*

Linden has long since jumped off the sofa and is busy running his tractor on the rug. He is satisfied and content with the wonderful story of the "sofa that speaks." I long for his free, childish spirit and quick faith to trust the God who does provide.

For some reason my spirit still feels heavy. I know from the year's experiences that life can hurt—its pinches go deep. Though God does give us the desires of our heart, sometimes in His infinite plan, He shatters our dreams and takes the desires of our heart from earth to preserve eternally in Heaven. Even though it's best for us in the long run, we feel the sting of its earthly consequences.

"Oh Lord," I pray silently as the hum of Linden's tractor rolls rhythmically by and the silent, disturbing words of the hospital bill burned in my mind, "make the message of the sofa drown out all my doubts and fears."

# 29

## Seventeen Pounds of Cheese

*Ellen (Barnhart) Heatwole*

The day after I had gone to our sofa expressly to hear
its message, I was kneading bread. I pounded and
punched the dough, making sure the ingredients were
thoroughly mixed. Like the dough, my thoughts were
tumbling and rolling over each other. The positive, thankful thoughts were mixing with the unanswered questions
of how and why and what next. The mixing bowl of my
mind contained the turbulent dough of pounded and
punched issues, which screamed for solutions, but yielded
no neatly formed loaves ready for baking.

I just couldn't shake the gloomy shadow hanging over
me. Earlier I had forced myself to sing with my
preschoolers songs of praise to God, which sounded
cheerful but did not lift my inner shadows. Next we had
quoted Bible verses together. "All things work together

for good to them who love God, to them who are the called according to his purpose." "He careth for you." "The Lord is my helper, and I will not fear what man shall do unto me." "The Lord is my shepherd; I shall not want." "God is our refuge and strength, a very present help in trouble." "He shall feed his flock like a shepherd: he shall gather the lambs with his arm, and carry them in his bosom, and shall gently lead those that are with young." These blessed Scriptures, which had assured our little ones of God's kind and loving care, had been spoken. The comforted and contented children had moved forward in their play—singing as they used the sofa to build a train.

Still I kneaded bread, while I fought the terrible weight of despair. But now I felt even worse—I was a first-class hypocrite! I had presented a loving, caring God to my children. They believed and were blessed. In my head I believed too. But my heart refused to cooperate with my head. *Haven't I done all the right things? Why can't I have victory? God knows how desperately I crave it. He sees my efforts to discipline my mind according to Philippians 4:8. Where is the peace He promised? When will I find relief from this bottomless heartache? Why should I keep trying? Why be a hypocrite any longer? I may as well let the tears come and give up my brave front.*

And then I heard a car pull into the driveway. Help! I was in no shape emotionally to even go to the door. But I had to. I breathed a prayer for God's reinforcement both physically and emotionally. My knees literally shook as I wiped tears from my eyes while I forced my foot to take that first step toward the door.

I looked into the smiling face of a young girl who had helped us on several occasions. Her eyes shone brightly with the love of God. Her step was light and carefree. She fairly bounced with energy and good will. She warmly greeted my children, who had heard her and had come running to give her a welcome. I couldn't help noticing the contrast between us. My eyes were clouded and care-worn, my step heavy and forced, my hands still flour-sprinkled and sticky from kneading bread dough.

But her hands were reaching out to me with a big hunk of "yellow," which I didn't recognize at first. "Here's some cheese for your family," she said cheerfully.

"Well, what for? And where from?" I asked. I knew we hadn't ordered any cheese. I couldn't imagine why she would be bringing us cheese.

"My folks were in Ohio," she explained, "and they brought some cheese along back."

"Well, how much is it?" I asked, thinking about the next-to-nothing balance in the checkbook, but also knowing that cheese doesn't grow on trees.

"It's nothing. My family was thinking about you and thought maybe you could use some cheese since we have a good supply. You can use it, can't you?"

"Oh yes! Yes, we can," I stammered, realizing anew that this angelic girl was God's gift for my deep need this morning. "I just wasn't expecting anything like this, and I feel I should pay you for the cheese."

"Oh, no," she insisted. "We want to give it to you—to help out a little. We know you have many medical expenses with your children's needs. And now we have plenty of cheese, so we want to share."

"Well, thank you, and God bless you," I replied with deep feeling—more feeling than she could have ever guessed. "I've been having quite a struggle this morning and God has used you to meet my need."

She was soon gone, but the afterglow of her angelic spirit permeated the atmosphere of our kitchen for a long while. I was still dumbfounded. That was a big slab of cheese. *How much?* I wondered. I got the bathroom scales and weighed that hunk of gold. *Seventeen pounds! Seventeen pounds of cheese! That is no small gift.* My heart lifted in praise to God, who gives beyond sofas—yes, seventeen pounds of cheese.

I called the children together, and we had a praise meeting and thanked the Lord for sending us seventeen pounds of cheese. They were so excited. One after the other, they spoke up.

"God takes care of us, doesn't He, Mother?"

"We said this morning, 'The Lord is my shepherd, I shall not want.' Now He gave us cheese."

"Won't Father be tickled? He really likes cheese."

"Yes, indeed!" I agreed. "We are all tickled. We all like cheese, and it's good nourishing food for us. God was so good to send Naomi to us this morning."

With their hearts full of joy, the children were soon chugging along in their makeshift train over tracks of praise to the land of cheese.

With tears swimming in my eyes, I pondered as I shaped the thoroughly kneaded dough into loaves to rise. *How precious is our God, to send that gift of cheese to confirm His love and care for me, just when I so desperately needed a token of confirmation. No, that cheese won't pay the hospital bill—seventeen pounds of cheese won't meet that need at all, but that cheese speaks volumes to me. It is a tangible proof of God's love to me. And to think, it came through a channel I would never have expected. Naomi and her family were sensitive to God's direction to meet our need. Oh, thank You, Father.*

# A Message From Heaven

*Eleanor Schlegl*

Eight years passed before I was able to see the "big picture" clearly enough to write this story. It began on Thursday, January 24, 1974; I was a parochial grade school teacher. My eleven-year-old daughter Karen and I both had the flu and were at home. Remembering her few requests for Christmas presents that year, I asked if she wanted anything special. She said she had always wanted a baby sister and had prayed for one.

"When you grow up, you'll probably have a baby girl of your own," I replied.

Little did I know that Karen would never grow up. She only lived three more days.

Karen's flu got worse. Saturday she was hospitalized. My husband Bill and I were not alarmed because she had been hospitalized twice before with a sore throat and flu and recovered quickly both times. But Sunday when she went into numerous convulsions in rapid succession, she was moved to the intensive care unit of the hospital.

Bill and I went to the coffee shop, realizing for the first time the seriousness of the situation. Even then we didn't think about her dying, but rather that we would have a rough night ahead of us.

When we returned to the intensive care unit, we stood gaping at the scene before us. Behind a glass enclosure were doctors and nurses dressed in green, starting Karen on an IV. I heard a voice say, "Those are the parents." Quickly the curtains were drawn, and a nurse ushered us to a waiting room.

We had been praying ever since the first convulsion, but I was in such turmoil that I felt as if I were getting a busy signal from God. I didn't seem to be getting through to Him.

Our doctor told us they finally had a diagnosis—Karen had viral encephalitis. Every nerve and muscle in her body was infected, including her brain. Since there was no medicine for this, she was in critical condition.

The last time we saw Karen alive was only for a minute. Her blue eyes were open, but she did not respond to us in any way. She looked peaceful. I wanted her to fall asleep so badly. I thought sleep would help her recover.

We returned to the waiting room, where we received a phone call from my father in Chicago. While talking to him, I heard, "Code blue, code blue," repeated over the hospital intercom. Hospital personnel rushed from all directions into Karen's room. I told my father I'd call him back, and we began praying again.

This time I felt an inner peace. I could imagine Jesus in the room with Karen, taking her by the hand as He had taken the hand of Jairus' daughter. Then our doctor came and told us he was sorry, but Karen's heart had gone into ventricular fibrillation. The doctors and nurses had done everything, but they could not save her. Sunday afternoon at 2:00 p.m., Karen died.

Everything had happened so fast; it was hard to comprehend. Just the week before, this girl had played volleyball.

During the weeks and months that passed, we went through the usual stages of mourning that follow the death of a loved one. Our son Bill Jr. was a nine-year-old at the time and feeling like a "forgotten" child. We tried to give him a lot of attention to assure him we cared about him too.

One day while I was cleaning my bedroom, I found a little cardboard circle with a smiley face drawn on it. In Karen's handwriting was written, "Smile, Jesus loves you." On the other side were the words, "To Mom and Dad." It was as though she had left this message for us.

Yet in spite of all these comforting thoughts, I began to seriously doubt my faith. That gravesite was such a reality; I wondered if Heaven really existed. Were we all just conning ourselves into believing something that could cushion the shock when tragedy struck? It seemed to me Heaven was too good to be true.

We felt the guilt connected with losing a child. *If only I had taken her to the doctor sooner. If only I had not taken her out on such a cold day. Why didn't we stay at the hospital the night before her death?* I thought I would bear this guilt for the rest of my life. The comfort given by my friends and relatives could not take it away.

But God always has a way of helping us through a difficult time. One thing restored my wavering faith more than anything else. I was unexpectedly pregnant with the baby sister Karen had prayed for. All of a sudden I knew God cared about me. The God I was teaching children about through Bible stories touched my life and spoke comfort to my heart when I needed Him most. The words "Smile, Jesus loves you" really meant something now.

I was strongly impressed with the reality that, whether it is life or death, God is in charge. He sent His Son so we can be free of guilt. I could stop blaming myself for what happened. The guilt I felt belonged at the foot of the cross.

From the very beginning, I could understand that this new life was being sent as a gift from God. Now I could accept the fact that God had allowed the older child to be taken away, and she is, indeed, with Him in Heaven.

On November 1, 1974, Kristi Ruth was born. We again have four in our family. Today our daughter Kristi has Karen's room, sleeps in her bed, and rides her purple bike. God sent her into our home to fill the void.

It was not always easy to start over with a newborn baby. But I thank God He cared so much that He gave us another opportunity to raise a precious child for Him.

After all, all children are His. He only lends them to us for a little while.

# 31

## Sorely Tried, But Safely Married

*Waneta Sandlin*
*As told to Norma Plank*

During my mission service in Kentucky, Hubert Sandlin, a young Christian from the community, won my heart. We set our wedding day for April 9, 1955. We decided to be married in Kentucky since a new church house had been built with more room than in the one-room schoolhouse where we used to meet. Also, the people of Newfound did not own cars and would have been unable to drive to Ohio for a wedding. We had also invited guests from other states, and even other areas in Kentucky, but cars could not be driven back to Newfound.

We had to figure out some sort of transportation for those who were unable to walk and for families with small children. So mules and horses were hitched to wagons and the two jeeps from the two mission stations were used to transport people. For some of those who had never experienced such primitive travel or walking over a very long swinging bridge, it was very scary, but for others it was novel and interesting.

The wedding day dawned bright and clear. It would be a full day with much to do. The two mission stations and the local people willingly prepared the meal. The day would also hold some disappointments, problems, and trials.

My grandfather Gabe Brunk had agreed to marry us, and I was looking forward to seeing him and Grandma. But when my parents, Rudy and Emma Brunk, arrived, they said Grandma wouldn't be able to come because Grandpa's brother had died suddenly. Grandma did not feel able to make the rough trip to my wedding and then leave immediately for her brother-in-law's funeral. I was disappointed, but I knew Grandma was frail and needed to be careful.

The second problem was that a men's quartet made up of Paul Smith, Edwin Hartman, Paul Hartman, and Richard Ross from Elida had agreed to sing at the wedding. But just shortly before the wedding, Richard Ross was rushed to the hospital with appendicitis. With no telephone service back in those hills, they were unable to ask us who we would want for a replacement. They chose Carroll Shenk, and the singing went very well.

So far the problems were minor, but the next one was potentially devastating and could have ruined the whole wedding day.

My papa was driving the jeep hauling people from the swinging bridge to the church. He was on his way out to pick up Grandpa when he saw Grandpa walking toward him on the narrow road. Carefully Papa began turning the jeep around. Those brakes on the jeeps often didn't hold because they were wet from driving through water so much. When the jeep was crosswise in the road, Papa pushed hard on the brake pedal. But the brakes didn't hold, and off he went, sailing down a steep hill toward a six foot drop off into a rocky creek bed. Grandpa watched in horror as his son whizzed down the steep hill. Just before going over the cliff, the jeep came to an abrupt halt against a small tree. Carefully, Papa eased out of the jeep as it wobbled against the little tree. When he reached the road, father and son praised and thanked the Lord for His miraculous protection. Papa stayed within sight of the jeep while Grandpa walked the 2½ miles to the church. Grandpa was very pale when he arrived.

When I saw him I wondered, *Why is he walking, and where is Papa?*

His first words were, "Rudy went over the hill."

I gasped, but breathed a sigh of relief when Grandpa explained what happened.

I was deeply grateful that God had prevented an awful tragedy on our wedding day, and He had kept my grandma at home and spared her this added stress.

The last problem came as Beulah Hartman, one of the bridesmaids, was pressing her dress for the wedding. A younger girl walked by the ironing board while shaking a bottle of shoe polish, which had a loose lid. The lid flew off and the black liquid splashed out onto Beulah's dress.

"Please, don't tell Waneta!" someone exclaimed. "She's had enough stress."

So I didn't find out until the stain was washed out of the dress, and it was properly ironed.

Well, the day was beautiful; the wedding took place; the singing was wonderful; and the food was delicious.

Because of the disabled jeep, more of the guests had a real workout, walking out of Newfound to their parked cars, and then traveling to their homes in various areas and states.

It was a wedding that was not soon forgotten. After the wedding, some of the neighbors hooked their mules to the marooned jeep, while Ezra eased himself behind the steering wheel and brought it safely up onto the road. I can't tell you if there was mechanical damage to the jeep, because Hubert and I were off on a simple but enjoyable honeymoon.

The day was memorable. Through it all I sensed the peace of God in my heart. I learned anew that God is able to help in every time of need.

# 32

## *Discerning God's Will*

*Norma Plank*

When I was in my middle teens, our church was blessed with two mission-minded ministers, Brother Elmer Yoder and Brother Lloy Kniss. Brother Lloy had spent a number of years on the mission field in India, and his many stories helped stir mission interest.

Missionary fires began burning in our church, and a committee was chosen to locate a place to send a missionary family. After much prayer, the committee felt led to investigate poverty-stricken areas in Kentucky.

Because most of the local people were too poor to own cars, many little stores were scattered along the main roads. Each store sold groceries, dry goods, and animal feed. People walked to the one nearest them for their supplies. Many of these stores had a little caged-off space in a corner for a "post office."

The mission committee was investigating near Oneida when they became thirsty and stopped at Lily Hacker's store for a drink. Lily was curious about these strange men.

"Where did you come from and why are you here?" she asked.

"We are searching for God's leading in planting a new church in some needy area."

Lilly's eyes lit up with anticipation. "Well, we shore do need the Gospel preached right here," she exclaimed. "Fact is, me and some other women have been gettin' together regular-like and prayin' that God would send someone to preach to us. We're a needy bunch of people. Tell you what I'm willin' ter do. I'll give you land ter build the church. Will ya come?"

The men were overwhelmed. God was making His will plain through the words of this gospel-hungry woman.

"Thank you for your generous offer, Mrs. Hacker," one said. "We'll report to our church at home, and I feel sure you will be hearing from us soon."

When our church heard the news, we were excited and ready to move ahead. Soon a church building was erected on Lilly's property. Merlin and Esther Good's family moved there to serve in that community.

Lilly Hacker was one of the first church members, and many more followed her example.

# 33

## Help in Time of Need

*Waneta Sandlin*
*As told to Norma Plank*

In my twenties I helped in the home of Ezra and Vida Good, a missionary couple in Newfound, Kentucky. We had no electricity, no running water, no phone service, and had a "path" instead of a "bath." To get from one place to another we had to either walk or drive the church's four-wheel-drive jeep.

One weekend Ezra and his wife were gone, and I was left alone with their five children. After we were all in bed and the children fast asleep, I lay awake, unable to sleep. It was hot. We had left the front door open, hoping for a bit of fresh air. The screen door had no inside hook to keep out unwelcome guests.

I believe the Lord kept me awake for a reason. *I'm sure glad Marion and Norma gave me this powerful flashlight. Since I can't flip on an electric light, it's handy to have a flashlight close by in case I need to check on the children.*

Suddenly, I heard men's voices, and they sounded close by. *I sure hope they don't come here,* I thought, straining every nerve to hear. *Oh, no, they're coming up on our porch! Now they're sitting on the porch swing; I hear it squeaking. Oh, Lord, help me! What will I do if they try to come in?*

There was nothing to keep them from coming right into the house. The unfastened screen door opened right into our living room, and immediately to the left was our bedroom. The bedroom door was also wide open to catch any nighttime coolness. From where I lay I could see through the bedroom door to the front door, which was discernable in the dim light. But what was that? Did I see a man's shadow in the doorway? My heart thumped.

Snatching up my trusty flashlight, I quietly sat up in bed, straining to see. *Are my eyes playing tricks? Surely, this can't be happening to me. Yes, the screen door is opening, and a man is coming right into our house. He's stealing in like a burglar, plus I can smell liquor from his breath. Oh, Lord, show me what I should do. Should I throw something at him?*

Then suddenly, I knew what to do. I shone a strong beam of light right into his face. "What are *you* doing in here?" I shouted loudly in what I hoped was a commanding voice.

Blinded by the bright light, the man couldn't see me at all.

"I . . . I want some matches," he stammered.

"You go out on the porch," I said sternly, "and I'll get you some matches."

I wasn't anxious to give matches to a drunken man, but neither did I want to rile him up by not granting his wish. I had learned to be very careful when dealing with these people when they were intoxicated. They could get very angry and do terrible things.

He staggered back outside, and I went to get the promised matches. When I handed them to him, he said, "I reckon my vehicle is 'bout to slip off da side of da road over yonder. It's right on da edge, ready to roll down into a big drop-off. My buddy's asleep in da back seat. Will you come out and help pull with your jeep?"

"You better wait until morning, and then get someone else to help you," I said, "because I don't know how to pull with the jeep."

"Well, at least you can come out and talk awhile," he urged.

"No, I can't do that, because it's two o'clock at night."

I was thankful he didn't insist. I returned to bed, but I could hear the men blundering around on the porch and talking. Finally, all was quiet and I drifted off to sleep.

I have always felt the Lord kept me awake that night and told me what to do. Isn't it wonderful that we have a God we can entrust our lives to? What a mighty God we serve!

# 34

## Pennies From Heaven

*William Schlegl*

*God provides, in one way or the other.*

Eleanor and I started our married life forty-six years ago as underpaid parochial schoolteachers. Though we had little income, we knew we were bringing the Word of God to all those little children, and that was enough to keep us enthused.

From the outset of our marriage, Eleanor and I agreed that I would handle the finances and bill-paying chores. Both our paychecks would go into the same account, from which we would pay our bills. I made sure the Lord's offering was always paid first, and He made sure there was always enough money for our family's needs.

After twelve years of teaching in parochial schools, I applied for a job in the public-school system. I knew that religion was off-limits in public schools, but I felt I could serve the Lord there too, if only in small ways. This turned out to be the case.

Sometimes, for example, I referred to church or Sunday school when writing a spelling sentence on the chalkboard. Often, this would prompt one or more of the students to eagerly talk about his or her church or Sunday school.

Although we never became wealthy, we always had food on the table and were able to pay our bills. When our son Bill Jr. needed a car for college, I made a deal with him. I would pay his insurance premiums, if he would handle all the other car expenses.

One evening not long afterwards, I was at my basement desk doing the bills. When Eleanor came down to announce that supper was ready, she noticed my frown.

"What's wrong, Bill?" she asked.

I hesitated, reluctant to answer. "I can't pay all the bills this month," I replied meekly. "Billy's car insurance of two hundred and fifty-two dollars has put me over the limit. I don't know what to do."

Eleanor looked over all the papers and bills and checks and envelopes scattered across my desk. Then she noticed a check sitting off by itself. "What's that?" she asked.

"Our offering for the church," I explained.

Her face lit up happily and she said, "Bill, you've always paid our offering to God first, and still do. He won't forget you. He's taken care of us all these years, and He's not about to stop now. Something will happen to help you pay Billy's insurance."

I tried to smile and say something positive, but all I could muster was a wan, "Let's eat."

The next day at school, I was still distracted by Billy's car insurance bill. I needed a miracle. Then one happened.

As I was diagramming something on the chalkboard, the assistant principal walked into the room. This was not unusual, for he made a point of visiting the classrooms regularly. The students and I just went about our business.

But this time the assistant principal didn't stay. Instead, he walked over to my desk, placed an envelope on my plan book, smiled, waved, and walked out.

My curiosity soon got the best of me, so I gave the students some quiet work to do while I sat at my desk. I carefully opened the envelope. To my utter disbelief and delight, I found a check from the school district, payable to me, for 252 dollars.

Apparently, as a result of the last teacher-contract, certain faculty members had been awarded a special raise. But the district had neglected to enact the raise. . . . until now!

As things turned out, the amount owed me, retroactive to the time of the contract, was precisely the amount I needed for Billy's car insurance.

Some would say this was pure coincidence. Eleanor and I would say it was the Lord answering our prayers and telling us, "You have been faithful to Me, and I want you to know I am faithful to you."

We are continually reminded that whatever we give to Him, He gives it all back many, many times over in one form or another.

# 35

## God Leads His Dear Children Along

*Condensed from a transcription of a talk by Ella (Greider) Yap*

As a young girl, I was slow and shy. One teacher wrote in my book, "If silence were gold, Ella would have riches!" It was only the Lord's doing that I accomplished anything.

My mother was born in Virginia, but her family moved to Ohio where she met and married my dad, Oscar Greider. We had no family worship, but I know my mother and dad prayed together. Sometimes when we were supposed to be in bed, we would sneak to the dining room and see them kneeling in prayer. I also knew my mother was reading through her Bible.

In 1933 C.C. Kulp was holding revival meetings in our community. One night I felt the Lord was asking me to stand up for Him, but I didn't. I went to bed that night thinking, What if the Lord would come back tonight? I promised the Lord that the next night I would stand. I did, and have never been sorry.

Toward the end of the meetings, Mother didn't feel well enough to go. A few days later she had one of her spells, and we had to call the doctor. He said we girls could go on to school, but a short time later an older cousin came and gave us the sad news that our mother had died. We cried all the way home from school. Beulah was fourteen. I was twelve. And Clara was ten. Our aunt and uncle, who had no children, came to stay with us for a while.

For several years different ladies came to help in our home. In 1938 we girls were shocked when Daddy told us he had married the last woman who had been working for us. Her name was Ida Mae Severs, and all she knew was bookkeeping. She didn't know how to cook; she didn't know how to clean, but she and Daddy seemed to get along with each other. Daddy and my stepmother had one son, Ben Greider.

After the ninth grade, I dropped out of school and began working out in people's homes. When I was older I did voluntary service work in different places, helping for a while in a hospital, at a children's home, and at a summer camp. For nearly a year I helped a missionary family in Kentucky. Then I was hired by Scottdale Mennonite Publishing House in Scottdale, Pennsylvania. I really enjoyed the work.

That's where I became acquainted with deaf people. Several deaf people worked at the publishing house, so church services were started for them and other deaf people in the area. A deaf preacher came and offered sign language classes for anyone who wanted to learn. I joined the class. The first song we learned was "Happy Day."

The deaf had a social meeting one Saturday a month, and I would help with the food. I also helped with a camp for the deaf.

The Mission's Director for the Deaf came and talked about their work among deaf people in Jamaica and their need for workers. But I was satisfied with my involvement with the deaf in Pennsylvania, plus I enjoyed working at the publishing house.

But all at once I had a change of mind; it must have been the Lord speaking. *Maybe I can go to Jamaica and work at the deaf school and maybe be a cook,* I thought.

After I talked with the director about it, he said, "Why don't you first go down for a ten-day visit to look it over and see if you still want to go."

I did, and was convinced that was where God wanted me to serve. As I returned home, this thought went through my mind: *People will think I'm crazy when they hear what I'm planning to do.*

First I had to get pledges from people for my support. When I got back to work, one of the ladies said, "Why don't you let some of us workers support you?" They began saying how much they would give. I didn't ask anyone for support. People kept coming to me. Some said they would give me five dollars, some ten, and some twenty each month. My brother, Ben Greider, was living at Harrisonburg, Virginia, at the time. He called and asked about my trip to Jamaica. After I shared with him about the work, he said, "I'll support you."

I said, "Ben, there are some workers here at the publishing house who have promised some help, but you may give the rest."

I was thrilled as I watched God working out the details without my asking for one cent. I knew it was the Lord's doing. Down through the years, He had prepared me—a quiet, shy girl—for working with the deaf.

In 1963, just before Christmas, I flew to Jamaica. With me I brought gifts for the deaf children. The children were so poor they hardly had anything to call their own, and they were very delighted with their gifts.

Instead of being the cook, I was asked to teach a class of four beginners. The youngest was fourteen and the oldest twenty. They had never been to school; they didn't know A from Z. I enjoyed teaching them. One day after a Bible lesson, I asked them if they wanted to accept Jesus as their Saviour. Two of them did—a girl and a boy. I told the missionary, and he made sure they understood the way of salvation. I was thrilled.

Most of the time I attended church services at the Deaf Center. But if the nearby Mennonite church where my cousin was pastor was having special meetings, I would go there. During one such meeting, someone said, "Amen!" good and loud. I asked my cousin who he was. "That's Edgar Yap," he said. Edgar was Chinese and really loved the Lord.

After I had been there a couple times, Edgar contacted me. He had lost his wife a couple years before, and he needed someone, but I wasn't interested. When he came to the Deaf Center to see me, I would sometimes hide until he left. The deaf girls would get after me. They liked when he came, because he would usually bring bananas or other things. Finally I agreed to meet him at a park. I went there and waited and waited and waited. When he finally arrived, I wasn't in the best of moods. Of course he apologized. He was a businessman and had been held up making some deliveries.

Our friendship went on for several years; finally I agreed to marry him.

I returned to the States for a few months to get ready for our wedding. One of the men Edgar bought produce from said, "She's not coming back; no, she won't come back."

But I did come back. And we got married at Edgar's house. Edgar prepared a Chinese dinner for 175 people. On the day of the wedding, I drove down the mountain to pick up a couple of deaf girls. On the way down, my brakes gave out and I nearly ran into a lady. I thought, *What if I don't get back in time for the wedding?* But I did and our marriage took place as planned.

After we were married, I helped Edgar in his store. His store wasn't doing well financially, because some of his employees stole from him; plus he was softhearted and extended credit to people who didn't pay. Before long, Edgar lost his business.

Not long after we were married, Edgar and I moved into the guesthouse at the Mennonite Church and took care of guests. But in a few weeks, the Deaf School asked if I would help there again, which I did. Before long the guesthouse was needed for a missionary couple, so we moved closer to the deaf school.

The deaf would often come to visit. Edgar couldn't understand sign language and sometimes he thought I was spending too much time with them. But I loved the deaf and couldn't turn them away.

When Edgar lost his business, he bought merchandise and went around selling it from his car and later from a van. Edgar really loved the Lord. He talked about the Lord and sang about the Lord. You couldn't talk to him more than five minutes till you knew he was a Christian.

I encouraged Edgar to move to the States where jobs were easier to find. In 1973 we moved to Florida and both found jobs.

One day in 1975 he came home from work, sweating and hurting. I gave him a drink, and he lay down. I went on with my sewing while he rested. Suddenly I heard a noise. I hurried to his side, but he was gone—dead of a heart attack.

After Edgar's death I returned to Jamaica and worked with the deaf again for seven more years before moving back to Virginia.

Maybe you're wondering what became of the boy and girl who became Christians soon after I first went to Jamaica. I don't know what became of the girl, but the boy came to the States and got a job making pottery. Once he visited me and brought a gift of pottery. He told me he had heart problems and his doctor wanted to operate, but he refused because he said he was ready to die. A short time later he passed away. One soul is worth more than the whole world, and I rejoiced that the Lord could use a shy person like me to lead him to the Saviour.

One of the deaf couples moved from Jamaica to Norfolk, Virginia, where there was a church for the deaf. The deaf couple's daughter could hear and speak, so with the daughter's help, I keep in contact by phone. Recently I received a card from them, which said, "We appreciate everything you did for us." That was a special blessing from the Lord.

If I had never gone to Jamaica, and had, instead, continued my work at the Scottdale Mennonite Publishing House, I would no doubt have a lot more in my bank account. But, though there were difficult times, I wouldn't trade those experiences for anything. I thank the Lord for the opportunity to go to Jamaica.

As I look back over my life, I marvel how my Lord gently led me step by step; yes, even a quiet, shy person like me, who enjoys speaking with my hands rather than with my lips. The Lord is worthy of all praise and honor—for without Him we can do nothing.

# 36

## God Provides Healing

*Nelson and Florence Heatwole*

On July 27, 1956 Nelson and Florence Heatwole were
blessed with the birth of their third child, Brenda
Faye. When Brenda was about three months old, Florence
noticed her dear daughter was refusing to eat and, of
course, not gaining weight. Very concerned, her parents
made an appointment with a pediatrician.

After carefully checking Brenda, the doctor reported
that she had a blood problem and swollen lymph nodes in
her neck and under her arms. He said nothing could be
done at the present for little Brenda. Florence was devastated. *How will I be able to drive home with such a heavy
burden on my heart?* thought Florence.

God saw this grieving mother as she walked dazedly
out to her car, clutching her precious little one. On her
way home she felt God's wonderful presence speaking
comfort to her, helping her drive safely home. She parked
beside the field where Nelson was working and waited for
him to arrive on the tractor. Then she poured out the

terrible news. As they wept, they wondered, *Can it be that our gift from God will not be with us much longer?*

"This is all the doctor gave me," said Florence hopelessly, holding up a small bottle of liquid drops. The medicine was to be added to Brenda's formula to increase her appetite.

During this same week the Peake church was having revival meetings. Before the service began, Nelson met with several other members for prayer. With a heavy heart, Nelson shared their little daughter's health needs. Earnest, fervent prayers ascended to God's throne in behalf of little Brenda.

The Lord heard those prayers; He reached down and touched their little one, and she was healed. All praise to God! It was entirely the Lord's doing and marvelous in their eyes!

Today Brenda is a loyal minister's wife and the mother of two healthy boys.

# 37

## God's Providential Care

*Nelson Heatwole*

The Monday after our son's wedding in Georgia in
1984, we were leaving for our home in West Virginia. We
stopped in Waynesboro, Georgia, to mail a letter at the
post office.

Some of our family were in another car following
us, so we parked on a side street. To get to the post
office, I needed to cross the highway. I looked both
ways and saw the street was clear to the left, but a
pickup truck was coming from the right. I waited for
it to pass; then, failing to look again to my left, I
started to run across the street with the letter in my
hand.

*Wham!*

Something struck me hard, spinning me sideways and
knocking me to the pavement. I had run into the side of a
moving car. Though bruised from the impact and the fall,
I picked up my letter and, looking both ways, crossed the
street and mailed it.

When I came back, my wife said, "Nelson, you need to go talk to those ladies parked next to the curb over there. They are very upset."

What could I say? I was the one who was hurting, but it had been my fault. I went to their car, thankful it hadn't been damaged. But the ladies inside the car, especially the driver, were nearly hysterical.

"I'm sorry I caused this accident," I apologized to the crying women. "Is there something I can do for you?"

Shaking her head, the driver said, "I think I'll be all right after I calm down."

Since there seemed to be nothing I could do for them, I returned to our car. After rejoining my family, they said how terrible and helpless they felt as they saw me run directly into the side of the car.

God spoke to all of us that day. We were shown in a real way that our loving Father has our days numbered—not only our days, but also our hours and minutes and seconds. If I had started across the road just one second sooner, I could have been severely injured or killed. I was reminded that God's guardian angels are encamping round about them that fear Him, and He is able to deliver them—even when we're unintentionally careless.

This happened twenty-three years ago, but I still express heartfelt thanks to my heavenly Father for His providential care. *Praise His Name!*

# IV.

GOD SPEAKS THROUGH

*Nature*

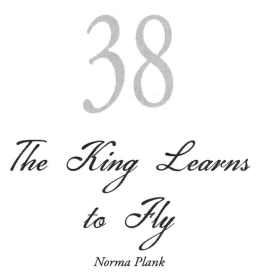

# 38

## The King Learns to Fly

*Norma Plank*

The great strength and courage of eagles earn them the name, "King of the Birds." The adult bald eagle of North America is dark brown with white tail feathers. The feathers on the head and neck are also white, giving it the appearance of a bald head. Eagles have a wingspan of seven to eight feet. They build their nests, called aeries, on high cliffs or on very tall treetops, providing a wide view of the countryside. The nests are huge; the outsides are made of rough, sharp branches and sticks, but the insides are very comfortable, with soft grass and leaves.

Five weeks after the mother eagle starts sitting on the eggs, the eaglets break through the eggshells. Wearing coats of fuzzy down, the hungry babies keep their parents busy feeding them. Soon their coats begin to change from fuzzy down to dark brown plumage. When the young eaglets are about eleven weeks of age, they are old enough for a change. Up until now, they have had a very nice, easy life. They were safe in a comfortable nest with Mama and Papa bringing them plenty of food. Now the food supply becomes less, and Mama begins pulling apart their nice, cozy nest. The nest is no longer comfortable, so they get out and look down over the face of the cliff. They don't know it, but they have some very exciting and scary days ahead. Very soon they will enter flying school.

Now when the parents fly toward the nest, the eaglets beat their wings, teetering on the edge of the nest, and scream for food, but time after time their food providers come with empty talons. The eaglets grow thinner. When the parents fly away, the eaglets pull at dried carcasses lying about the nest and pick at them. The loss of their baby fat makes them quicker in their movements and at times, while flapping about in their excitement, they become airborne for a moment or two, hardly touching the nest. Now and then a parent gives them a little food.

Now the eaglets no longer have a parent brooding over them for night-time warmth. Hunger and cold are having an effect on the eaglets, not only on their bodies, but also on their dispositions. The frosty air ruffles their feathers and chills their bodies. As the morning sun casts its first rays on the side of the aerie, the eaglets flap their wings and bounce to the edge to take advantage of the warm rays. For a moment, they find themselves airborne. They are now light, firm-muscled, and ready for flying school!

On the first day of school, they see Mama eagle coming toward them with outspread wings. The eaglets start screaming for the food hooked in Mama's talons, but she zooms right past the nest; then Papa eagle zooms very, very close with a marmot, exciting the hungry eaglets into a frenzy. One eaglet forgets his fear and leaps for the food. Over the edge he goes—tumbling, tumbling, beak over tail feathers, wings flapping in panic, and his heart pounding wildly in his chest. The rocks below are coming toward the eaglet at a terrible speed. Just at the last second, the eaglet gains control of his wings and glides across the valley, making a scrambling, almost tumbling landing on a bare knoll. The immediate danger is past— what a relief! Papa eagle zooms by and drops the marmot close by. Half running and half flying, the eaglet pounces on it and enjoys the feast.

A similar performance is repeated time after time until the young eaglets learn to fly very well. In this way they are being prepared to face life. Without this very difficult experience, they would never be able to take their place as "kings" in the bird kingdom.

God spoke to me through this little story. Sometimes, like the mother eagle, God allows me to go through scary and difficult times. Then I cry out, "Lord, this is too hard. Please, don't make me go through this!"

Just when I think I will crash on the rocks below, my dear Lord gives me the wisdom and strength I need and says, "My dear child, I won't take your problem away. You need this experience, but I'll go with you and supply your every need; I'll take you safely through. Just trust Me. I'm preparing you to become a 'king' and 'priest' in My Kingdom."

I believe God is more interested in developing my character than He is in my comfort. He wants me to learn more about faith. He wants my character to be formed in His likeness. I rest assured that a time will come when I will look back and say, "That hard experience was just what I needed. It has strengthened me in my walk with God."

*But they that wait upon the LORD shall renew their strength; they shall mount up with wings as eagles; they shall run, and not be weary; and they shall walk, and not faint.*

Isaiah 40:31

# 39

## A Lesson From a Fish Ladder

*Ashley (Bonvie) Plett*

The sun highlighted the tips of the pine trees as my friend and I walked along a seldom-traveled path to a dam built "in the middle of nowhere." The dam was an impressive structure. It had a bridge we could walk across and easily observe both sides.

As I knelt and peered through the bridge grating, I saw a thought-provoking scene. Dozens of trout were valiantly fighting against a stream of water flowing down a fish ladder. The fish squirmed, leaped, and flopped their way to the top, after which they would disappear for a moment only to be swept down the ladder in utter defeat. They tried again and again.

How futile! Had the fish only moved a few feet to the left, they would have discovered an opening that was calm and level. But they simply refused to look elsewhere. They fought their way up in their own strength, only to face defeat.

As I meditated on this pathetic scene, I considered how often my missions are as futile as the attempts of these fish. How often I follow my own way in my own strength, rather than seeking help from God!

I asked myself, *Do I want to fight my way up all by myself, only to find that the path which seems right will end in utter destruction?* No, the only right path for me to follow is God's—the strait and narrow way. That is never futile; for if we follow His way, we can have a happy, fruitful life here that will end in the glorious home above, where we can sing His praises throughout all eternity.

# Twenty-Nine Years in Prison

*Norma Plank*
*Rewritten by permission*

Recently I visited a smiling, bright-eyed old man. He had spent the last twenty-nine years in a Chinese prison because he was a pastor. To survive that experience is a miracle in itself. Many times he was beaten and asked to deny Jesus. He would always reply, "I'd rather die than deny my Lord." Then they would throw him back into his cell to die. But God had other plans.

In spite of his long prison term, this man had such a healthy glow that we wondered how it could be. "How could you maintain such good health while spending twenty-nine years in prison?" we asked.

He surprised us by saying, "Because I got to eat all I wanted."

We asked, "How could that be possible?"

He said, "When I was in prison, I received watery soup without much nutrition. One day while I was praying, I said, 'God, it would be so nice to eat eggs.' I forgot my prayer, but four days later I opened my eyes wide. There in front of my mat on the floor was an egg. It was much bigger than the eggs I had seen in the market. Could it possibly be real?

*"I must be dreaming,* I thought, so I pinched myself. It hurt, so I thought, *It must be a real egg—maybe it's a goose egg. But what was a goose egg doing in my cell?* I picked it up. It was real! I looked around but could find no clue as to how this egg could have gotten here. I didn't look long, though, for I was extremely excited and very hungry. I made a hole in the egg and sucked it out clean. After eating so much watery soup, the egg tasted delicious.

"When I finished eating the egg, I thought deeply about what had happened. Surely God doesn't answer a prayer such as I had prayed. I hadn't really asked for an egg; I had only expressed the longing of my heart.

"When I woke up the next morning, there was another egg in the same place. *This is strange,* I thought, *God must have sent it. I wonder if God will repeat it three times.* So now I prayed, 'God, would You give me an egg for a third time?' And the next morning I found another egg.

"The fourth night I stayed awake to see who was bringing eggs into my room. Perhaps a sympathetic guard, who was a secret believer, had heard my prayer and was risking his life to bring the eggs into my cell. At about three o'clock in the morning, I heard a light scratching noise on the floor. I did not move. A mouse was using his nose to push an egg through a hole in the wall. I hardly dared to breathe. The mouse pushed the egg to the same spot where the others had been placed. Then he sniffed around a bit and left. The mouse was storing his stolen goose eggs in my cell!

"This went on for many days. One fall day I was thinking that it must be apple season. My mouth got watery from thinking about eating an apple. So I prayed, 'God, if You can give me eggs, how about an apple?' What do you think happened? Yes! God used a different mouse to bring me an apple every day during the apple season. You know, the apples the mice chose were the sweetest ones, even though they may have had some bruises.

"While hateful men were trying their best to destroy my faith, God was reminding me of his power and faithfulness. All of my remaining time in prison, I was fed by little creatures sent by God. How I praised Him. Nothing is too hard for God."

# 41

## A Valuable Nuisance

*Wendell Hochstetler*

A pleasant light glowed over the supper table as the young family enjoyed their meal. Suddenly some uninvited guests appeared, swooping around the light overhead, dropping to the table, and sometimes into the food.

"Oh, Wendell, those bugs are such a nuisance," groaned Mother. She rushed for the electric sweeper, and soon the offending creatures were sucked out of sight.

But Father observed that as the bugs were sucked up, others were always ready to take their place—they seemed to be everywhere! His poor wife seemed to be fighting a losing battle.

The bugs sometimes irritated Father also. One day he was fixing a cup of hot chocolate. He had dumped some chocolate mix into his cup of hot water and had begun stirring when he noticed what looked like a lump of cocoa. He continued to stir to no avail; and when the lump refused to be crushed by his spoon, he knew it was a bug. How disgusting!

Those bugs seemed to be everywhere. *How many have I eaten already?* he wondered. *Can bugs do anything besides irritate people? I think I'll look in the encyclopedia and check this out. Maybe I can use it for an object lesson.* Sure enough, the encyclopedia showed a ladybug that looked nearly like our uninvited bugs. They said fruit growers love ladybugs. In the early 1900s, ladybugs from Australia were introduced to California to aid in the fight against cottony cushion scale insects on the fruit crop. Ladybugs are very beneficial. They eat not only scale insects, but also plant lice and other harmful insects.

Father couldn't deny that while some bugs can be a nuisance to many people, they may be doing a great work behind the scenes. Suddenly God graciously revealed a lesson that he could learn, even from irritating bugs.

His thoughts went something like this: *Sure enough, I can apply this to my life. What about the "bugs" or hardships in my life? Do I see the benefits they bring, or do I snap them away and wish they would never come? Just because unpleasant happenings set me back in my desired goals, and they may cause irritation, that doesn't mean they do no good for my inner man. I'm convinced that everything God allows in my life, He intends for a good purpose. Without a doubt, God's purpose is that these irritations will help me become more like Jesus. "Lord, help me to be more thankful for all that You allow in my life."*

*My brethren, count it all joy when ye fall into divers temptations; knowing this, that the trying of your faith*

*worketh patience. But let patience have her perfect work,*
*that ye may be perfect and entire, wanting nothing.*
James 1:2-4

*And not only so, but we glory in tribulations also:*
*knowing that tribulation worketh patience; and patience,*
*experience; and experience, hope: and hope maketh not*
*ashamed; because the love of God is shed abroad in our*
*hearts by the Holy Ghost which is given unto us.*
Romans 5:3-5

*Many shall be purified, and made white, and tried.*
Daniel 12:10

# The Uninvited Wedding Guest

*Norma Plank*

Some fifty years ago in the hills of Kentucky a wedding was held. At that wedding a never-to-be-forgotten incident took place—a miracle, in fact.

People walked to the wedding from different directions—down the roads, across the fields, and over swinging bridges. Finally they were all assembled in the church. Brother Paul Smith, the visiting minister, was sitting on the platform.

Christian weddings were very happy and serious events then, just as they are today. But just as the ladies' quartet was about to sing, a commotion began. Children giggled, women lifted their feet off the floor, and men stretched out their long, denim-clad legs this way and that, banging their heavy work shoes down with heavy thumps on the bare floorboards.

Brother Paul, facing the audience, had a ringside seat. He soon discovered the cause of the commotion. A very frightened mouse scampered this way and that, trying to escape those clumping work shoes. Brother Paul was noted for his keen sense of humor, but he knew this was serious business. The wedding party would soon be coming down the aisle! What would happen if that mouse ran across the aisle just in front of the bride?

Then he saw one of the singers give a little jump. Had the mouse run across her foot? The startled girl bravely stayed at her post.

Brother Paul knew something must be done. So he did the only thing he could do—he prayed. *Lord, You created this little mouse, and You can make it behave. Please take care of this distraction.*

Not even he could have imagined how God would answer his prayer. The frightened mouse obeyed his Creator; he scampered to the front, scrambled up the steps to the platform, and hunkered down, facing the audience—right beside Brother Paul's chair.

All during the sermon the little mouse stayed put, until Brother Paul had finished and returned to his seat. Then the two sat there side by side, one on the chair and the other on the floor by those kindly feet that meant him no harm. This uninvited guest witnessed the whole wedding, and when the last "amen" was said, he scampered quietly away to his hole in the baseboard.

Jesus worked a miracle at a long ago wedding in Cana. God also performed a miracle at a wedding in Kentucky.

The heavenly Father cares for His children, and hears their calls for help.

# 43

## The Ant's Amazing Antennae

*Tom Anderson*
*As told to Norma Plank*

Have you ever watched a colony of ants work? This insect group works beautifully together. How do they do it? Do they use sign language? The following story indicates that ants somehow communicate with their antennae.

Tommy was a ten-year-old boy from Dayton, Ohio, who often watched a hill of common black ants near his house. He observed the entrance to their hill and the special trails the ants followed. One day an ant came struggling up the trail, carrying a bread crumb. Tommy wondered what the ant would do if the entrance were blocked, so he dropped a small stone over the entrance.

Soon the ant bumped up against the stone. Finding it could not enter, the ant dropped its load of bread at one side of the trail. Then it hurried over to the stone and, with its antennae, felt all over the obstacle as though measuring it.

Next it scurried over to another ant. They stood face to face, tapping their antennae together for some time. The first ant proceeded to find another ant, and they also went through the same tapping procedure.

Each of those two ants persuaded two more ants to come to the rescue by also using the antennae-tapping method. Eventually six new ants arrived to help the first ant with its problem. Those seven ants surrounded that stone and, *pronto*, they removed the obstacle from the entrance.

The six recruits went back to their business, and the first ant marched over to its bread crumb, lifted it up, and carried it through the entrance.

Now what do you think? Do ants talk? Do they use sign language? We can't be sure, because we're not ants. But we can be absolutely sure that they do an excellent job of communicating by using their antennae, which in turn causes their work to go well.

The Bible says we should consider the ways of the ant and be wise. God can teach us many spiritual lessons through this marvelous creature. What are some lessons we could learn?

1. Seek to work peacefully with others.
2. Be humble enough to ask for help when you need it.
3. Don't be lazy.

4. Help those who are in need.
5. Don't give up when things look difficult.

These are a few that God spoke to my heart. No doubt you can think of more!

# 44

## The Sunflower Parable

*Norma Plank*

I enjoy gardening, so, naturally, I can't tolerate weeds. One morning while washing the breakfast dishes and viewing my garden I received a jolt when I saw a big, robust weed poking its head above the row of green beans.

After finishing the dishes, I marched out with the intention of jerking out that offending weed. However, a close-up view showed no weed at all—just a beautiful, husky sunflower. I had no experience with sunflowers. How did it get there? I hadn't planted it. Maybe a bird was responsible for dropping the seed in our garden. It looked so strong and healthy that I didn't have the heart to jerk it out.

Day by day that sunflower held my attention as it swiftly shot up and the trunk expanded. Soon the flower head began to form. One morning I noticed the head was slanted to the east. Was it going to die? I investigated, but it appeared healthy enough.

That evening, to my great amazement, the same head was slanted in the opposite direction. What was going on? Here was a mystery to solve. I watched closely. The head was again slanted toward the east the next morning; it pointed straight up at noon; and it slanted toward the west in the evening. The mystery was solved. Of course! It was a "sun" flower—that's how it got its name.

That sunflower was obedient to the sun's directions. Its obedience continued for some days, but all the while the head was swelling in size. Finally the day came when that sunflower was taller than any garden plant or any person, and it had become so "bigheaded" that it refused to take directions anymore. The sun continued to move across the sky as usual, but the sunflower would not budge or even lift its face.

The Lord used this sunflower to speak a lesson to my heart. As long as I follow the directions given by the Son, I can remain spiritually healthy. But if I let pride enter my life and refuse to take directions from the Son, I am asking for serious trouble.

In like manner, the sunflower was in for trouble. One night there was a rainstorm. The next morning when I viewed my garden, that huge sunflower was broken over and its head was touching the ground. Instead of presenting a haughty appearance, it looked deeply humbled. Before long the sunflower was dead.

Soon afterward the birds were flocking around, receiving nourishment from the seeds. The next spring there were many new sunflowers popping up from seeds the birds had missed.

Again the Lord spoke a lesson to my heart. If I would bear fruit for the Master, I need to humble myself and die to all selfish desires. Then I can be used to bring nourishment to others, and new souls will be born into the kingdom.

# Prodigal Pigs

Earl and Viola Schlabach
*As told to Norma Plank*

Brother Earl leaned over the fence, looking at his fifty pigs. He raised his cap and scratched the bald spot on his head. "Say, if you fellows keep growing like this, you'll soon be ready for market." Noticing the activity of one industrious pig, he shouted, "Oh, no, you don't! I caught you that time." Brother Earl hurried over to repair a place where the pig was making a hole under the fence.

At the supper table, Earl said, "Viola, I outsmarted one of the pigs today."

"How did that happen?" she asked.

"He was making a hole under the fence, and I repaired the damage just in time. They're a nice-looking bunch of pigs and will soon be ready for market." A smile of satisfaction creased his weathered face as he dipped gravy onto his mashed potatoes.

"I surely hope they don't get out," sighed Viola. "We both know there is no farm animal as contrary as a pig on the loose."

"Don't worry, I plan to keep a close watch on them," assured her husband.

A few days later, Earl heard a commotion and rushed out onto the back porch. His mouth dropped open as he looked toward the pigpen. Two of the fence panels were pushed slightly apart, and pigs were streaming through the opening. Several headed for the road, some started for the woods, some scurried behind the barn, and some began rooting in Viola's garden and flower beds.

Earl hurried up to the pen just as the last three were about to make their escape. He'd need to widen the opening if he ever hoped to get those pigs back in, so he swung one panel back and said to the remaining three, "Come on; you fellows may as well kick up your heels with the rest of them." Out they bounded, squealing and frisking their way up to join the others in the woods.

Earl stood and shook his head; the situation looked hopeless. He had tried to be so careful, but there they were—fifty pigs romping here and there. Then he noticed a few down by the road. *First,* he thought, *I had better get those off the road.*

"Here, Samson," Earl called to the faithful dog. Samson came running, tongue hanging out and eager to help. "Let's get those pigs off the road, Samson."

They hurried and finally had the pigs closer to the house but certainly not headed for the pen. Earl mopped the sweat from his brow and said, "Come, Samson, let's get a drink." He filled a pan with water and set it down for the dog. Then he walked dejectedly into the kitchen to get a drink of water for himself. There sat Viola and their married daughter, Rachel, enjoying some mother-daughter time together.

Viola looked up from her sewing and asked, "Are you having trouble?"

"Yes, the pigs are all out of their pen. How will I ever get them back in?" *Surely Viola will offer to help me,* he thought.

"Rachel and I will be praying for you," was all she said.

Earl glanced out the window and then rushed out the door, shouting, "They're on the road again!"

With Samson's help and a great effort from Earl, they managed to herd the pigs toward the house again. Exhausted and discouraged, Earl dragged himself up the steps and leaned against a porch post. *Why didn't Viola offer to help me? That's not like her. It was fine to offer that she and Rachel would pray, but I need her help. I'll never get those pigs back into their pen.*

Suddenly, right in front of Earl, there appeared a most unbelievable sight. Pigs began coming from the woods, from the garden, from around the corner of the barn, from the flower beds, and from the road—all heading in one direction, toward the pigpen. Into the pen they went.

Earl hurried out, swung the fence panel shut, and counted. Yes, all fifty pigs were there. He pulled his hanky out again, this time to wipe tears.

"My Lord," he prayed, his shoulders shaking, "I've just witnessed Your great power. You have spoken volumes to me through those pigs. I thank You so much! It was an impossible situation for me, but not for You. You've made me aware once again that there's nothing too hard for You."

After wiping a few more tears, he thoroughly checked for any additional holes in the fence. Then he hurried to the house to thank his wife and daughter for the help they had given—by praying.

# V.

## GOD SPEAKS THROUGH A STILL

# *Small Voice*

# 46

## God Is All-Powerful

*June Bontrager*

One evening in August of 1990, my husband Edwin and I sat at the supper table with our family of eight children, who ranged in age from two to twenty-two years. One topic of discussion was our anticipated trip to Bay Tree in Alberta, Canada, for the weekend where Edwin had agreed to have meetings. Often when he and I visited there, the children stayed home. This time we planned to take them all along for an extended family outing. Little did we know that God had different plans.

As we ate, we enjoyed typical family conversation and laughter. Our daughter Susan remembers thinking, *What if something would happen so that our family could never sit around the table again like this?*

Supper over, we scattered to begin packing for our weekend trip. The evening would be a busy one. My husband and our oldest son Dave took our van to a neighbor's garage to do some last-minute work on the exhaust system.

Sometime later, someone knocked at the door. The phone rang at the same time. I went to the door while one of the girls answered the phone. At the door stood Merlin, a member of our church and also Edwin's business partner in construction for twenty-one years. While talking to him, I was summoned to the phone. Placing the receiver to my ear, I heard my son's voice. "Mom, there's been an accident. Can you come?"

I said, "Is it Dad?"

"Yes," he answered.

"I'll be right there." My mind was reeling as I hurried back to the door. *Is my husband still alive? Why didn't I ask Dave more about it?*

As I relayed the news to Merlin, I suddenly remembered I had no transportation.

Merlin said, "I rode my bike, but I'll hurry home and get my truck. I'll be right back to pick you up."

He hurried away, and I explained to the children that their father had been hurt in an accident. I tried to ready myself for whatever lay ahead. When Merlin returned, I urged the children to pray and then left to face the unknown.

Soon we were at the shop. As we hurried past the big open door, I noticed a pool of blood on the floor.

Dave met me. "Dad is in the house and alive," he said. "But he's badly hurt. He was under the van, holding a portable grinder about a foot away from his face, when the grinding wheel broke apart and a large piece flew into the left side of his face. Another piece ripped through the side of a five-gallon pail. Danny, another church member, had stopped by and was holding a trouble light for Dad when it happened. Danny was showered with disk fragments, some of which drew blood."

We hurried toward the house. *How would Edwin look?* I wondered, cringing at the thought of what I might find. Stepping into the kitchen, I saw my husband sitting in a chair. He was very pale, and the left side of his face was covered with a big towel and an ice pack. Because his mouth was injured, he couldn't talk clearly. I was greatly relieved to see him alive, but my heart cried to see him hurt so badly. The wife of the mechanic, an emergency room nurse familiar with traumatic injuries, was giving him first-aid until paramedics arrived. God was watching over us!

Time crawled until we heard the welcome approach of the ambulance, its siren screaming. After the paramedics sized up the extent of Edwin's injuries, they called for a second ambulance—one that was better equipped. By this time our daughters, Roseann and Evelyn, were on the scene. Evelyn remembers carrying Dad's shoes and thinking how strange it was to see her hard-working father injured and lying on the stretcher. We were deeply thankful for our children's support.

After the second ambulance wailed its way to us and its medics examined Edwin, they considered calling Life Flight because of severe head injuries and an unresponsive left eye. Edwin's wish was to be transported by ground if his injuries were not life-threatening.

My thoughts were fragmented and questioning as I rode in the ambulance to the hospital. Certainly there would be no enjoyable family trip to Bay Tree. Instead, the picture included a badly injured husband, a hospital, doctors, and frightened children at home alone. I hadn't actually seen the injury, but having been an LPN, I understood the descriptions—"severe lacerations to the face," "blown pupil," and so on. The driver, a lady, chatted with me for most of the hour's drive to one of Portland's best trauma centers. Exchanging conversation helped me keep my emotions in check.

At the hospital emergency room, Edwin was whisked off to be examined more extensively while I was questioned by hospital personnel. Time dragged as I wandered up and down the hall, awaiting permission to go to my husband. Three people came to be with me—our son Dave; Danny, who had held the trouble light; and Edwin's father, Ernest Bontrager. As the hours dragged on, I became concerned for Edwin's elderly father, so I suggested that he and the others go home. I felt God's presence and strength and wasn't apprehensive about staying there alone.

Sometime later a nurse told me I could go to Edwin. Walking toward his room, I again wondered how he would look. I thought I had prepared myself, but I was shocked at what I saw. The piece of grinding wheel that struck him had made a deep slice through the left side of his face, affecting his nose, mouth, cheek, and chin. I wondered how any doctor could put his face back together. Would he ever look the same again? Would his eye need to be removed?

I braced myself for however long I would need to be with Edwin at this stage. I asked the Lord to please help me be strong . . . over and over . . . while I swabbed the oozing, gaping wound, soothed his forehead with a cool washcloth, and helped him when he was sick from swallowing blood. This went on for five hours while specialists were called to do specific exams. I felt sorry for those doctors, who were being aroused from their sleep. Several CAT scans were taken and read before any surgical procedures could be started. During those five long hours, only once did I feel a bit light-headed.

At 2:45 a.m. Edwin was finally taken to surgery, and I went downstairs to a waiting room. Thankfully, the large room was deserted. I thought I would try to sleep. Instead, as I sank gratefully into a soft chair, my pent-up emotions gave way to a flood of tears. It felt so good to cry and pour out my heart to the One who knows and cares about all our troubles and fears.

During the long night I remembered something that had occurred about two weeks before. In his Sunday morning message, Edwin had encouraged the church family to take seriously the prison ministry we had begun. "We are entering Satan's territory," he had said, "and we can expect attempts to hinder our efforts." He also said, "I refuse to be intimidated by Satan's assaults." Hearing him say that had sent a fearful chill through me. Later in the day I had told him my apprehensions that he might be called to prove that statement.

Now I wondered, *Is this accident Satan's attempt to get Edwin out of the way? And this isn't the first time Edwin's life has been threatened. Besides,* my tired brain rambled on, *a bishop ordination is being planned for our congregation next month to replace our present bishop, who is in failing health. Is this Satan's design to put Edwin out of the picture?*

Many were my unanswered questions that night. I determined that whatever God's will was in allowing this accident, I would do my part in submitting to His plan.

As the welcome daylight slowly filtered through the waiting room windows, Dr. Nolan, a kind and caring plastic surgeon, came into the room. Still dressed in surgical blues, the doctor sat down and carefully explained the extent of Edwin's injuries. He said the piece of the disk had caused an injury similar to that of a gunshot wound as it plowed through the tender facial tissues. The three-hour surgery revealed that the flying fragment had knocked out an upper tooth, broken a quarter-size piece of bone from the orbital socket of his skull, and severed nerves on its path through the left side of his face. There were extensive nose and mouth injuries too.

The surgical team had scrubbed out many tiny bits of black material from the abrasive disk that had been embedded in the tissues. There was the possibility of losing vision in the left eye. Dr. Nolan also noted that a "higher power" had been looking out for Edwin. "A little higher, and the fragment would have penetrated his brain; a little lower, and it would have severed his jugular vein," he said.

Hitting the tooth had slowed the deadly force of the fragment. I realized again what a wonderful heavenly Father we serve.

Finally I was allowed to be with Edwin in the recovery room. As I watched him resting peacefully, I was amazed and very grateful. Dr. Nolan had done an expert job at closing the gaping wound. Edwin's face was "grotesquely swollen," as one of the children said later. But over a period of time the swelling would be gone, and the damage to his physical appearance would pale in light of the fact that Edwin was still with us.

That evening, the children came to the hospital to see their father. Daughter Bethann remembers that Dave huddled his siblings outside the hospital room to remind them that Dad would look different. Soberly they filed into his room and stood around his bed. Their father was very tired, but so glad to see all eight of them. We prayed together before going home, and high on the list of praise was thanks to our heavenly Father for sparing Edwin's life.

On the ride home with the children, I listened as they talked freely about their feelings during the evening of the accident. They expressed their disappointment about not going to Bay Tree, but uppermost were the many fears and uncertainties they had endured. How badly was Dad hurt? How much longer would they need to wait for more news? How was this going to turn out?

Then we discussed how God had taken care of so many minute details relating to the accident. God was definitely in control. As I took part in the conversation and answered the many questions, it was a soothing balm to hold two-year-old Nolan on my lap after a two-day separation.

When the children were all in bed, I settled gratefully in my own bed, hoping to sleep off some of the weariness and emotional stress. But sleep eluded me as I lay thinking about the events of the past two days. I couldn't ignore the fact that I might have been a widow this very night, left alone to care for the children. My thoughts tumbled on and on. What was God telling us? Would we learn the lesson He wanted to teach us through this experience?

Suddenly a verse came to mind, the words of Jesus to His disciples many years ago. "All power is given unto me in heaven and in earth." Right on the heels of remembering that precious verse, a still small voice said to me, *"I allowed this accident to happen, but I controlled the path of the disk fragment."* Yes, that was so true! My mind went back to what Dr. Nolan had said about a "higher power" and how close the call had been. I thanked God again for His sovereignty and His providential care.

Several factors stood out as I began counting my blessings. Edwin was not alone when the accident happened; it had occurred where an experienced nurse could give him immediate care; Merlin was at our door when the call came, and he provided a way for me to go to Edwin; and the older girls were at home to stay with the younger children, so I could leave immediately. God had all those details in place! It was clear that we can trust our God implicitly.

Later Edwin shared some of his memories. "God gave me a constant awareness of His complete control from the very first moment after the accident. He gave me an overwhelming peace, which took away all worry about the outcome."

As extensive as his injuries were, Edwin experienced very little pain. When we asked Dr. Nolan about this, his immediate response was, "I think it was because of all the prayers being offered, your faith, your family support, and Edwin's positive attitude." We were blessed by his recognition of God's presence hovering over us.

The weeks and months following this incident were filled with doctor visits and four more surgeries. Our church family was very supportive, sharing tokens of love in the form of meals, cards, flowers, visits, and monetary gifts. We were especially humbled by the sacrifice of Jim and Vickie Bechtel, who are dear friends from Idaho. They stayed a month with us, taking care of our children, keeping the household running smoothly, and filling in for Edwin at work while he recuperated.

In the sixteen years since the accident, the main physical adjustment for Edwin has been to live with severely impaired vision in his left eye. We love to count our blessings when we reflect on this event. Certainly God's mercy and power were shown in preventing a tragedy and in giving Edwin an extension of time with us.

# 47

# *The Nine O'Clock Prayer*

*Miriam (Breneman) Shank Coblentz*

One morning before she was married, my mother Mabel was alone in the house washing dishes. Suddenly she had a strong urge to pray for her widower father, Frank Bear.

Obeying the Holy Spirit's prompting, she left her work, went to her bedroom, and dropped to her knees. After praying fervently for her father for a time, she felt at peace. Then she went back downstairs and continued her household duties.

When Frank came in for lunch he said, "Mabel, something strange happened this morning."

"What was that?" she asked.

"Well, I was having some trouble with the machinery I was pulling, so I got off the tractor to see if I could fix it. While I was working on it, I noticed that the tractor, which was parked on an incline, had started rolling back toward me. I was sure I would be knocked down or crushed between the two machines, but suddenly the tractor stopped. How I thanked the Lord!"

Mabel asked, "What time did this happen?"

"Around nine o'clock."

That was the very hour when Mabel had felt the strong urge to pray for her father! With awe and gratitude she hugged this precious experience to her heart. God helped her that day to take a giant step forward in faith. She learned how important it is to obey the Holy Spirit's prompting immediately.

# 48

## Does God Still Work Through His People?

*Leonard Shank*

My father was the third son in a family of four boys and one baby sister. The youngest boy was Elijah Shank. We called him Uncle Ligy, and he had a large family of all boys. When we were children, my father and Ligy often got together in each other's homes and played musical instruments. We thought Uncle Ligy played very well, whether guitar, mandolin, violin, banjo, or piano.

The problem was that he would play music when he should have been working. As a result, he got behind financially. This caused much stress between his family and ours as the years went by. In addition, they lived careless lives. Eventually our families drifted apart. Uncle Ligy lost the family home place and moved about eighty miles to Culpeper, Virginia, to work on someone else's farm. As the years passed, we had less and less contact. Our feelings toward Uncle Ligy's family were really not as they should have been.

Forty years later my father had passed away, and all his other siblings were gone except Uncle Ligy. Then I heard that Uncle Ligy was hospitalized with cancer and not expected to live.

The next Saturday my wife and I decided to go see him. I dressed in my plain suit and took along my pocket New Testament. But I also took along the wrong attitude I had developed against Uncle Ligy over the years.

When we found Uncle Ligy's room, I hardly recognized him. How he had changed! I tried to have a conversation, but with the TV turned up loud, his daughter-in-law in the room, and a nurse going in and out, Uncle Ligy was pretty distracted. I had his attention only long enough for a parting prayer.

On the way home, I thought, *Well, I tried; I have done my part.* I dismissed Uncle Ligy from my mind, or so I thought. My wife and I both expected that we would be going to a funeral in several days.

Unknown to me, God had His own plan, and He wanted me to be part of it.

During the night, I awoke with Uncle Ligy on my mind, and I was prompted to pray for him. God helped me realize that Uncle Ligy was not being arrogant or aloof, but was simply afraid to die and did not know what to do about it. I knew the Lord was asking me to go again and speak with my uncle.

Now it was time for me to get my attitude corrected. This was accomplished with much prayer over the next several hours. I was made to understand anew that "Jesus saves"—not just me. In fact, I am not the one to pick and choose who will be saved, because Jesus died to save *all* people.

I was the Sunday school superintendent at the time. Early the next morning, I called and made arrangements for someone to take my place so I could go to Winchester. I also asked for special prayer from the church for me and for Uncle Ligy, because many of our people knew him.

When I got to Uncle Ligy's room, the door was closed except for a small crack. I gently pushed it open far enough to see inside. The TV was turned off, and Uncle Ligy was lying in bed with his eyes closed. I thought he was asleep; but he heard me, looked my way, and asked me to come on in.

After some small talk, I pushed the door shut and got right to the point of my visit.

I was again dressed in my plain suit; so moments later when a nurse pushed the door open, she excused herself when she saw me. She told me to let the nurse's station know when I was finished. Isn't it wonderful how God arranges things? My uncle and I were alone with God.

I said, "Uncle Ligy, you're going to die. Are you ready?" He said, "No, and I'm scared!" He burst into sobs.

Then I asked, "Uncle Ligy, has your pastor been here to talk to you about your relationship with God?"

"No," he sobbed. "I haven't been in a church since

Fanny died. We don't have a preacher, nor do we go to church."

"Uncle Ligy, you once knew the Lord," I gently reminded him, "Do you believe God is able to forgive your sins?"

There were more sobs and a long pause. Finally he said, "I don't know. I didn't always treat Fanny like I should have, and I cheated your dad. They're both dead now, so I just don't know."

God has promised to give the words we need in times like these, but often the Bible is the best, and that was the case here. We read some Scriptures and talked about the many things in the past that troubled him. He finally came to the conclusion that, yes, Jesus did die for him; and yes, He could and would forgive him—even for these very sins.

Then I asked, "Uncle Ligy, do you want to invite Jesus into your heart right now?"

"Yes, but I don't know how."

"I'll help you, if you want me to," I offered.

He was very ready and said, "Yes, I want that."

Uncle Ligy prayed after me as I prompted him, "Dear Lord, I acknowledge that I am a sinner and I need Your forgiveness. I know that without Your forgiveness, I face Your judgment and eternal death. I believe You love me and You showed Your love by sending Your Son, Jesus Christ, to die for my sins. I trust in Him alone to put me in a right relationship with You. I ask You to take over in my life and live within me. I know I am not worthy of this, but I thank You for it. In Jesus' precious name I pray. Amen."

I am convinced that Jesus did, in fact, come into his heart, because Uncle Ligy was immediately a changed and peaceful man. But he seemed exhausted, so I gave him a New Testament with salvation verses marked and left.

Before noon the next day, he was moved to a nursing home in Harrisonburg, Virginia, about eight miles from my home. Early on a Tuesday morning, I went to see him again. Uncle Ligy had been reading the New Testament that I had given him. However, he was hardly able to speak, and it was very hard to understand what he said. By that afternoon, he was unable to communicate with the nursing staff at all. Early Wednesday morning he went to be with Jesus.

That this story ends so well is certainly due to the mercy and work of God. First, God prepared both me and Uncle Ligy for our Sunday morning meeting. Second, I have many faults, failures, and shortcomings. I don't want anyone to think that I am better than I really am. Remember, I had many opportunities over the years to talk to Uncle Ligy and Aunt Fanny, but I didn't take advantage of them. In fact, to my knowledge no one— including me—ever talked to Aunt Fanny about her salvation. I deeply regret this. Third, it was by God's will and to His glory that these events unfolded as they did. God gave me the mission to carry out; He willingly and lovingly forgave the sins of Uncle Ligy; and the host of angels in Heaven rejoiced in his salvation.

# The Organ Story

*Martha Martin*

My aging mother decided it was time to downsize, so she planned to have an auction. I immediately thought of the organ. Even if we got nothing else, I wanted that organ. Daddy had bought it years before especially for me.

About a month earlier, John Swartz had preached a sermon about living frugally. He gave illustrations such as the following: For fifty cents, medication can be purchased in India to treat one child's eyes for prevention of blindness. So every time you spend fifty cents for a soft drink instead of giving the money for this purpose, some child in India could go blind.

Now as the thought of the organ flashed through my mind, God seemed to say, "You don't need that organ." Though it wasn't easy, I yielded my desire to God.

On the day of the sale, I knew I wouldn't be bidding on the organ, but I was curious to see who would buy it.

Near the end of the day the organ was up for bids. The auctioneer started off at one hundred dollars and then quickly went down, as auctioneers do, to get a starting bid. When he said "five dollars," our youngest son Tim put up his hand. The auctioneer immediately said, "Sold! You need it." (All day Tim had been holding items up for the bidders to see.)

What a surprise that was! It was as if God gave the organ back to me! Yes, it's Tim's, but the organ will be here for me to use as long as Tim lives here.

The next morning I awoke about 2:00 a.m., and God seemed to say to me, "I was testing you as I tested Abraham."

I said, "Now You know I love You, Lord."

He replied, "And now you know I love you, Martha."

Later I told the auctioneer this story. He said that he didn't know why he knocked the organ off so fast, since he usually doesn't. Now he knows!

This was a wonderful experience. Thank God that He gave me the courage to be faithful under test.

# 50

## *Confession Brings Peace*

### *Donald Plank*

When I was about seventeen years old, a close friend invited me home with him for Sunday dinner. We were both Christians and members of the same church. My friend lived on a farm with a wooded area on the back side. After a good lunch, we decided to walk back to the woods.

A sawmill had been set up in these woods. We knew very little about operating a sawmill, but upon examination, we saw how to start the motor and figured out which levers would move the carriage that carried the logs past the large circular saw blade. I think I moved the levers, causing the steel head-block to move into the slowly turning blade. The result was severe damage to the teeth of the saw. Frightened, we quickly stopped the motor and left.

Some weeks went by and the sawmill was moved to another location, but all this time my conscience gave me no rest. God kept speaking to me. I couldn't read my

Bible or pray without thinking about what we had done. I told my friend that I couldn't live with my troubled conscience any longer and was planning to confess my sin. He offered to go fifty-fifty with any payment for damages that might be laid on us.

I finally asked an older church member who knew the sawmill owner if he would go with me to confess what we had done. He agreed, and we drove about ten miles to where Mr. Stimmel was operating his sawmill. We had to walk some distance into the woods to find him. My feet felt like lead as we walked along, because I knew this man was not a Christian and used foul language. Not knowing what he might do, I was scared. We found him sitting by a tree eating his lunch. The brother with me told him what we boys had done.

Mr. Stimmel told us when he saw the damage, he assumed it was done in revenge by a former employee whom he had fired. He said that if we boys would pay the eighty dollars it cost to repair the saw blade, he would be satisfied. In the middle 1940s, eighty dollars was no small amount for two unemployed boys to pay. What I remember most is the great relief. I felt as though I was walking on air as we headed out of the woods to the waiting car!

I'm glad the Lord kept prompting me about the sin in my life. A clear conscience is worth far more than any amount of money it may require to obtain it. I'm also glad to say that we finally paid off our debt and both of us are living for God today.

## 51

## *Help Me, Lord!*

*Norma Plank*

Are any of you women like me? If you were ever a widow, I'm sure you have gone through similar experiences. I was unaware that my husband, who had just died of cancer, had done so many things for me—things only men seem to know how to do. Oh, I knew he was good and kind, but I had taken so much for granted. Now I was a widow of one month, and I was learning many hard lessons.

My granddaughter Loreen came to keep me company for several months. In exchange, I would coach her in algebra.

One January morning Loreen and I went to the courthouse where I needed to take care of some legal transactions. Unable to finish, I was told to return the next day. The next morning Loreen stayed home to work on algebra.

"I shouldn't be gone long," I said as I left.

The morning was chilly with a drizzly rain. I pulled out of our driveway and up a steep grade. I was thankful

Houck Road wasn't icy. One winter we had needed chains for six weeks straight. We lived "back in the sticks," but we loved it.

I turned slowly onto Lincoln Pike. This road was covered with gravel, but it was a regular washboard. At thirty miles per hour, I vibrated my way over several miles when suddenly my car started lurching from one side of the road to the other. I had to wrestle with the steering wheel to keep the car out of the ditch.

I thought, *Oh, no! A flat tire, and I've never changed a tire in my life.*

I dreaded the idea of working in the rain, but I hopped out and was relieved to find that all four tires were fine. I got back in and cautiously moved forward, but the car still wobbled terribly. *It must be a tie rod,* I thought. *Our tractor acted like that when its tie rod broke.* I got out again and looked under the front of the car. Something strange hung there. Now what?

Feeling utterly helpless, I crawled back into the car, draped my arms over the steering wheel, and dropped my head onto my arms. Then I cried out to God, who cares for orphans and widows.

"Lord," I pleaded, "what am I to do? I can't drive this car, and I shouldn't leave it here in the road. I don't want to leave my granddaughter alone very long either. You've promised to care for me, and I need Your help."

Suddenly a great peace settled over me, and I felt complete assurance that God would provide for me. I raised my head and noticed a house a short distance away. I felt the Lord urging me to go there and ask to use the telephone.

God's peace went with me as I walked through the drizzle and knocked on the stranger's door. A lady came to the door, and I told her my problem before asking to use her phone.

After looking me over, she hesitantly let me come in and showed me her phone. First I called Loreen and told her I was having car trouble, but that she shouldn't worry; I felt sure the Lord would help me. Next I called each of our church families to see if any of the men were available to help. One after another, all the wives said they were sorry, but their men were not at home. I assured each one that the Lord would help me and they were not to worry.

The lady of the house, who introduced herself as Mrs. Miller, said, "I'm a woman of faith, but I don't have that kind of faith."

I assured her that the Lord had a plan, but I just had not found it yet.

Mrs. Miller looked out the window, and suddenly pointed at a barn some distance from the house. "What do you know!" she exclaimed. "My father-in-law, Bill Miller, must have just come from town, and he's at the barn right now. Why don't you go ask for his advice? He's very kind and helpful."

I thought, *Lord, do You want me to ask a strange man for his advice? I just wish the barn were closer to the house.*

Since this was the only door the Lord had opened, I accepted the suggestion and walked to the barn. There was a nice pickup truck, but no man in sight. As I peered through the wide cracks into the empty barn, I saw a man walking on the other side of the building.

Praying for courage, I took a big breath, and called, "Mr. Miller!"

He shouted, "Yes!"

"I need your advice."

His cheerful reply came immediately. "I'll be right there."

Shortly, an older man came striding toward me. He listened carefully as I explained my problem. Then he said, "Just get in my truck. We'll take a look at your car and see if it really has a broken tie rod."

After looking under my car, he assured me the tie rod was broken. "Now," he said, "I need a piece of wire to hold things together."

He had a topper on the back of his truck and inside he had wired up a nice rod for hanging clothes. He was just ready to dismantle it when an old rattletrap of a truck stopped and one of the two men in it yelled, "What's the matter, buddy? Are you having trouble?"

Mr. Miller said, "Yes, we have a broken tie rod, and I need a piece of wire to splice things together."

"No problem! There's plenty of wire over in that old barn. We'll get some."

Both men leaped from the truck, leaving it in the middle of the road, and sprinted across the muddy field to the barn. I wondered, *Are they stealing the wire?* I decided not to say anything; I just stood there and watched as God unveiled His plan.

Soon they were back and handed over a length of baler wire. We thanked them heartily. With a smile and a wave, they hopped into their truck and roared off down the road.

Mr. Miller soon had the tie rod wired up. "Now," he said, "you'll need to drive slowly and not take any sharp turns. Just follow me up there to my son's house, and you can call your mechanic. He'll probably take care of an emergency like this right away."

"But," I sputtered, "I don't know of any mechanic. When my husband was living, he took care of our mechanical needs."

"Don't worry, I know a real good mechanic who works on my vehicles. Would you like me to call him and see if he'll work on your car?"

"Oh, I would be so happy if you would." The Lord was at work.

After making the call, he came out smiling. "Mrs. Hartman, just follow me, and I'll see that you get your car safely over to the garage. The fellow said he has time to fix your car today."

"Oh, that's wonderful!" I exclaimed.

When I had parked my car at the garage, I expected to wait there until it was fixed. But Mr. Miller asked, "Did you say you were on your way to the courthouse to do some business?"

"Yes, but that can wait until another day."

"No," he insisted, "I'll take you there and wait in the truck until you're finished. Then I'll take you home, because it will likely be evening before your car is ready to drive."

"Mr. Miller, you have been so kind. I can't think of troubling you any further."

"It's no trouble at all. I want to do this for you."

I'm sure he could see I was hesitant. But he had been so kind, and I didn't want to hurt his feelings; so we were soon driving up to the courthouse. Forty minutes later, we were driving into my driveway to my house where Loreen was looking out the window.

"Now, Mr. Miller," I said, opening my purse, "I want to pay you for your kindness. You were the answer to my prayer."

"No, Mrs. Hartman, I won't take a cent. I am happy I could do that for you."

"Well, I thank you with all my heart." Tears were spilling from my eyes as I got out of his truck and hurried into the house.

I felt awe and wonder at the workings of God as I shared my amazing story with Loreen.

Several hours later a mechanic called to say my car was ready to be picked up. A sister from church took me to get it.

A church family is a wonderful gift from God. It means so much to be able to call on any one of them and know they will gladly help if they can. But truly it is the Lord Who is our help in any time of need—even though He may use some very unusual ways.

Yes, our Lord still speaks today, and He cares for His needy children.

## An Old Life
## Made New

*Chester Heatwole*
*As told to Norma Plank*

My wife Louise and I learned to know a lady in the Peake community who added spice to our lives by telling us her experiences. She had had a difficult life. Her non-Christian husband sometimes beat her up. I was told that passing neighbors sometimes saw her lying in the yard, and they didn't know whether she was dead or alive. It was just Fanny Hoover lying out there.

One happy day her husband became a Christian and began acting like one. Of course, he stopped beating Fanny. But Fanny was not a Christian, and she had a very good memory. She turned the tables and started beating him! She was really hard on her husband. Some people would say he was just getting a dose of his own medicine. So Fanny and her husband were both having a difficult life.

But there was another happy day when Fanny became a Christian, and then things took a turn for the better. After her husband died, her children made life hard for Fanny. They would entice their mother to get drunk so they could steal her food and take advantage of her in other ways. The children seemed to enjoy constantly making their mother miserable.

Fanny had become a member of our church. One day Franklin Burkholder, the deacon, went with me to visit her. We were sad to find Fanny drunk. The deacon and I felt her children might eventually cause their mother's death by keeping her drunk so much.

I felt prompted to call her doctor. I introduced myself and explained my concern, and then I said, "Doctor, I need your help. I want you to put Fanny in the hospital and 'dry her out' so she can come to her senses. I know she doesn't want to be this way."

The doctor said, "Well, I don't know. I just don't know about that."

But somehow God convinced the doctor through me to admit her to the hospital. It wasn't long until I heard sirens; the deputies and rescue squad were coming to take Fanny to the hospital. Fanny wasn't about to leave voluntarily; she did not want to leave at all. In fact, she used this as an opportunity to tell the Mennonite preacher where he was wrong. It felt like a severe whipping. Fanny went on and on about how terrible these Mennonite preachers were, but finally we convinced her to go to the hospital.

But before she would agree to go, she insisted on giving me a dancing lesson. Now I believe dancing is sin, but that mattered not at all to Fanny. She suddenly put her arms around my waist and tried to give me a dancing lesson.

The deputy just laughed. For myself, I thought about how sad it was to see what people do when they're drunk. They lose control of their senses and do very foolish things. God wants us to surrender control of our lives to Him.

The result of Fanny's hospital stay was good. I had a talk with her after she was "dried out," and she said, "I want to go back to church and get up and tell the people that I sinned. I'm sorry I ever did that." She also told me she felt bad about the way she had behaved toward me.

Finally she was released from the hospital. I think it was the very next Sunday that she stood in church and confessed her sins and received forgiveness. That was a marvelous day in Fanny's life.

Fanny had been introduced to snuff at six years of age. She came to like it and even thought she couldn't do without it. From time to time, brothers and sisters in the church would talk to her about her snuff habit. Fanny would try to quit, but it seemed that she couldn't give it up. So here she was, an old woman who had used snuff nearly all her life. Yes, she wanted to be rid of the habit, but she still liked the stuff.

The day came when she was taken to a nursing home because her health was failing. While she was there, God continued to speak to her through her conscience about her snuff habit. One day she decided to give it up once and for all. She experienced complete victory! Fanny lived long enough to prove her victory, and then she died. That was a wonderful testimony.

Fanny liked many Christian songs, but her favorite was, "I Have Decided to Follow Jesus." When we would sing that song, she would be affected so strongly that she would move physically. Her life was a testimony of that song. When she went to meet her Lord, she went with the anticipation of Heaven. I believe she's there right now.

Compiler's note: Brother Chester Heatwole passed away on September 4, 2005. I love to imagine that Chester and Fanny are looking into their Saviour's face with adoration and are praising Him, together with people from every nation and kindred, for His great mercy and love.

# Water for Evan

*Becky McGurrin*

"I want water!" cried Evan, for the changes in his routine had become almost unbearable. Like many autistic children, Evan longed to escape into a pool of soothing, *predictable* water.

So his mother prayed, "Dear Father, You hear his cry. Please lead us to a place where there is enough water to calm my boy's troubled spirit."

The church had asked Evan's family to move to a small congregation about two-and-a-half hours away from their home. Their one concern in agreeing to move was this: How would Evan handle all the changes? Any change is hard for a person with autism, and relocation would mean different people, different noises, and different trees. Why, even the ceiling would be different. So many "differents"! And for Evan, *different* meant the same as *scary!*

So his mother prayed. *Father, wherever You send us and whatever changes You bring are fine with us. But would You please grant this one small plea, for Evan? Just a small pool of water?* Mama prayed this prayer silently. It was a secret between her and God. Not even Daddy knew what she had asked for.

As she finished her prayer, Mama thought she heard the still small voice of God responding in her heart, "Evan shall have his water." With anticipation, she was now ready to join Daddy in the search for a new home.

"This place has potential," said Daddy as they drove up the lane to a house for sale in their new community. "It would be tight for a while, but we could add more rooms onto this end of the house."

"Perhaps," responded Mama as she silently looked around the lot. She thought, *Surely this can't be the place for us. There is no water, not even a small stream.*

"On second thought, maybe that mobile home closer to town would suit us better," Daddy said as he noticed the uncertain look on Mama's face.

"We'll see," she answered. Although the trailer did have a small stream, it wasn't really big enough for Evan to float in.

"Lord," Mama prayed again, "I've asked You for water for Evan, and I felt sure that You whispered a yes in my soul. So why is it that none of the places we've looked at have had enough water? I'm not sure anymore. I'm starting to feel both helpless and homeless. Where should we go, Lord?"

Only two weeks more, and they would be closing the deal to sell their current home—two more weeks, and they would be homeless. But God led them to drive up a mountain lane to a house just two and a half miles from their new church. The family grew excited even before they stepped out of the car. They all felt, *Surely this is it!* The view was absolutely beautiful. The house had plenty of bedrooms. It was clean and ready to move into.

Within an hour they had shaken hands with the banker who was selling the home. He promised that they could close on the property within two weeks. Hallelujah! With relief and great excitement they began the drive back to the "old" place to settle affairs there.

"But wait!" Mama said to herself, her mind in a turmoil. She hadn't seen any water on the property! "How can this be, Lord? I was so sure You had promised to have water waiting for Evan. Was I mistaken? Is this really the right place for us?" In confusion she questioned both herself and her God.

From the back seat, Evan's sweet voice broke into her troubled thoughts. "Mom, when we move, can I take baths in your bathtub?"

"Why sure, honey," she replied. "But why do you want to take a bath there when there is a bathtub right across from your new bedroom?"

"Because," he answered cheerfully, "your bathtub is so big that I could float my whole body in it at the same time. I would like that."

Tears welled up in Mama's eyes. She could picture the tub he was talking about. A *garden tub,* they called it. It was a full five feet long, three feet wide, and a foot and a half deep—a regular little indoor pool! She had never imagined when she asked God for a small stream or pool that He would provide them with such a lovely, private, indoor pool that Evan could use all year around!

*Oh, You wonderful Father,* Mama prayed. *It **was** Your voice that answered me when I begged You for a pool. How marvelous are Your ways! You give me so much more than I ask for. On the side of a mountain where there is no stream, only a God like You could have provided water for Evan! Truly I thank You.*

# 54

## *Am I Willing?*

*Martha B. (Yoder) Shank*

"Here they come!" Jane announced as the out-of-state car drove up the lane. "Now my world will extend beyond home. Voluntary service while caring for children sounds great to me."

Mother added, "And now you won't have to help with the cooking. It sounds as though you have it made."

"Don't tease, Mother. You know what a hard time I have with cooking."

Jane gave her mother a loving embrace before they began carrying her bags to the car. Soon they had all her things wedged in. Only a spot on the back seat was left for her.

As the three girls traveled mile after mile, Jane enjoyed the new scenery. She had never traveled much, and this was promising to be adventurous.

Anna and Dottie bubbled over, and soon Jane felt quite comfortable with them. After several hours, they stopped at a shady spot to eat the lunch Jane's mother had so kindly packed for them.

Dottie turned to Jane. "The VS unit needs a cook this year. How would you like that job?"

"Wh-what did you say?" Jane stammered in shock.

"I said you might get to be cook at the child-care center," Dottie answered. "At our last meeting in late spring, they mentioned that the new VSer would probably need to cook."

"But I'm going to work with children! That's what they told me!" Jane sputtered. "And I can't cook!" she gasped.

"When you go into VS, you have to be willing to do what is needed," admonished Anna. "Dottie and I had to do lots of tasks we felt unprepared to do. We had to learn by doing."

The subject was dropped as the threesome continued the trip to the home of Dottie's cousin in Virginia, where they would spend the night. As Dottie introduced Jane, she jokingly added, "Jane doesn't think much of her new job as cook for the unit and child-care center. They didn't tell her she would have to do that when she was accepted."

"Please, girls, I just can't cook! What will I do?" moaned Jane. "It's no joke, either."

Dottie's cousin tried to comfort her. "Jane, I don't believe God would ask something of you without giving you the strength and wisdom to do it."

The next morning, Jane explained the plan she had developed during her restless night. "I'm going to find a way back to Pennsylvania from here. That will be easier than trying to find a way home from Florida. I know you must think I'm a quitter, but I'd rather be humiliated now than go there to try doing something I can't do. I've always had a struggle with cooking, and I just can't do it!"

Anna looked at Dottie and then at Jane. "If you feel so strongly about it, I am sure something else could be worked out. We are sorry to have upset you so. We'd really be disappointed to leave you behind."

Somewhat comforted, Jane decided to continue the trip as planned.

After they arrived at the VS unit in Florida, the Lord allowed Jane a respite from the prospect of having to cook. Her first assignment was housecleaning at the minister's home. Next she made curtains for the huge nursery at the child-care center. Occasionally she helped the cook at the unit house prepare meals for the summer workers, but no one said anything about the cooking position that would need to be filled in the fall.

Several weeks later, the unit began gearing up for new workers and the busy season. Jane began to wonder who the cook would be. She completed the last day of cleaning at the minister's home.

As she cleaned the venetian blinds in the living room, the words of a hymn drifted to her from a record player in another room.

"I'll go where You want me to go, dear Lord,
    Over mountain, or plain, or sea;
I'll say what You want me to say, dear Lord,
I'll be what You want me to be."

—Mary Brown (1856-1918)

The Lord spoke to Jane. "Are you willing to be what I ask you to be? You say you want to be in My will. But My will for you may be cooking. Can't you trust Me?"

A battle raged in Jane's heart as she finished her work. "I just can't! And I don't want to cook!" With that, she suddenly saw the truth. It was not that she *couldn't* cook, but that she didn't *want* to cook. She wasn't willing to submit to God's will if it crossed her will. That was the root of her problem.

"Oh, Lord, forgive me!" cried Jane. "I realize You may want me to cook. I want to yield my will to Yours. And I know You will help me do whatever You ask. Oh, Lord, I *will* cook if I am asked, only because I know You will give me the help and wisdom I need. I do want Your will." The battle was over, and peace came at last.

Jane finished the housecleaning and then sat down to supper with the minister and his wife.

"Next week our whole staff will be here," explained the minister. "All the other girls were here last year and are trained for work in the nursery. Rosie has learned to be an excellent help in the office. Even though she cooked over the summer months, we will need her full-time in the office. Jane, could you possibly cook for us?"

In tears, Jane confessed the intense struggle she had just come through, of which the minister and his wife had been totally unaware.

Before they parted for the evening, the minister prayed, "All I can say is, Thank You, God, for Your faithfulness. You are always on time."

## 55

# God Always Makes a Way

*Vilas Amstutz*

When Charles Breneman became ill in the summer of 1986, I volunteered to service his lawn mowers and tiller. After Charles' death in 1996, I continued keeping the mowers and tiller running for his widow, Mabel.

Of Mabel's three children, her two married daughters lived in Missouri. Eight years after Charles' death, her only son decided to move away. By this time Mabel was eighty, and it was difficult for her to think of getting along with none of her children close by.

*How long will I be able to carry in wood for my heating stove?* she wondered. She prayed about it, asking the Lord to make a way for her.

My wife had passed away four years before, when I was seventy-five. In May 2004 I was working on a cranky mower for Mabel. She was troubled about her son and his family moving away.

I sensed God telling me to ask Mabel if she would be interested in going out to eat and visit. But she declined, saying she didn't think she ever wanted to get married again. Mabel felt that marriage would be too great an adjustment at our age. I assured her that her decision caused no hard feelings and that I would still consider her a friend and keep her mowers running.

I then felt led to say to the Lord, "I will not ask anyone else about becoming a possible companion; I will live here alone as gracefully as possible. But Lord, if You have other plans, the initiative will need to come from someone else."

In July Mabel reluctantly called and said both of her self-propelled, walk-behind mowers would not start, so I went again to help a widow in need. I found that she was more troubled over her son and his family's leaving than over two cranky mowers. I asked, "Have you considered moving to Missouri where your daughters are living?"

She said, "No, I want to stay at Elida."

I did not offer any suggestions or ask any more questions.

Several days later while Mabel was at her cleaning job at the doctor's office, she felt especially miserable. She prayed, "Lord, show me what to do." Suddenly the Lord revealed to her that He *had* opened a way for her, but she had turned it down. So she decided to call me when she returned home.

That afternoon my telephone rang. I answered, and the now-familiar voice said, "It's me." After some general small talk, Mabel asked, "Do you remember what you asked me back in May?"

"Yes, I remember."

She said, "I have been thinking about it, and the Lord has changed my mind. I was wondering if the Lord has changed your mind. Or maybe you have other plans or are thinking of someone else."

I said, "No. I'm only letting the Lord lead." I then felt free to ask her, "Are you interested and ready to pursue a possible friendship?"

Her answer was a strong yes. She seemed relaxed and delighted about getting together, and we had an enjoyable first date.

During our conversation, Mabel asked, "What do you think your children will think of us being together?"

"I can't be sure right now," I said.

Mabel had talked to her daughters about the possible friendship, and they had offered no objections. A bit later, she called her son. "Have you seen or heard of anything going on around here?" she asked.

"No, I haven't," he replied.

Then she said, "A Honda has found its way to my house a few times."

He caught on immediately, and Mabel sensed he was very pleased.

Soon after this, Mabel invited her son's family and me over for a snack after a Sunday evening service, which everyone enjoyed. As one of her granddaughters left, she gave Mabel a big hug and said, "I'm glad for you, Grandma."

The next day, the report that an eighty-year-old lady was dating an almost-eighty-year-old man was being discussed in areas from Virginia to Oregon and many places in between. Mabel also shocked the ladies at the doctor's office by telling them she was quitting her cleaning job and getting married.

On Sunday morning, November 28, 2004, our simple wedding took place after the Sunday school hour. We enjoyed a fellowship meal at our Christian day school building, with many relatives and friends attending. Some came from quite a distance for this "older couple's wedding."

Mabel came to live in my house. Can you imagine trying to decide what to keep and what to dispose from the accumulation of fifty years from two homes?

We are thankful for the health we have, and we've thoroughly enjoyed our first three summers with gardening and flowers.

"Thank You, Lord, for speaking through Your still small voice and supplying our needs by leading us together."

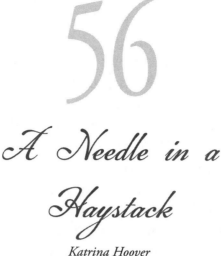

# A Needle in a Haystack

Katrina Hoover
*Some names and details changed for privacy*

It was a blistering summer in Brooklyn, New York, and two weeks of Bible school had just come to an end. The Bible school staff were sitting in the basement of the brick church on Atlantic Avenue, trying to cool off and sharing experiences. Two young men in the group, Anton and Jed, were eager to get back to their book routes that extended throughout New York City.

Suddenly the phone rang. Anton answered and then motioned for Jed to come.

"What's up?" asked Jed.

"Bad news, Jed. Ralph just called. He went down to pick up the book van, and it wasn't there."

"Not there?" asked Jed, eyes wide in surprise.

"Nope. It's gone! But maybe it was towed away by the police. I'll check that out before we report it stolen."

While Anton punched in the numbers for the police station, Jed stood quietly by and did a mental check. *I was the last one to drive it, but I'm sure I put the "club" (an anti-theft steering wheel lock) in place. I locked the van doors, and the keys are in my pocket. Yes, it was probably towed away by the police.*

Jed listened as Anton spoke to the police. "You haven't been towing today? Not at all? Well, I guess that answers our question." He put down the phone, looked at his friend, and said, "It's stolen, and I doubt we'll ever see it again."

For the three youths manning the New York City book routes, the loss of the van was a disaster. This was their primary vehicle, especially modified with shelves for their books. They had spent hours in it, going from one store to another to restock bookracks across the city.

The theft was reported to the New York Police Department, but no one was hopeful. Vehicles are stolen every day in New York, and few are ever recovered. The thieves had too many hiding places. Even if the police didn't have more important things to do, searching for a stolen vehicle in that huge city would be like looking for a needle in a haystack.

By Saturday morning, the van could be in another state. The book team knew they were powerless, but God wasn't. So the church people prayed.

Jed kept saying, "Lord, the van is Yours, and the book route is Yours. If it is Your will, You can bring the old van back to us."

By Monday morning, many people had prayed for the team and their van, but no one had seen a trace of it.

Using a borrowed van, Jed covered the route and returned home in time to be at Brother Jon's house for Wednesday evening prayer meeting. Jed again mentioned the van as a prayer request. Even though five days had passed since the theft, it didn't seem right to quit praying.

Kristie, a VS girl, glanced at Jed and asked, "Did you hear that Sister Rachel had an interesting thought about the van?"

"No! What and when?"

"Well, it happened while she was praying about the van. She got this picture in her mind of the van possibly being in Far Rockaway."

Jed stared. "You mean she knows where it is? Why didn't someone tell me this before?"

"I don't know. Maybe she decided it was just her imagination. You could talk to her."

"I think I will!" It didn't matter that the story sounded incredible.

Jed didn't wait until he got home. He pulled out his cell phone.

Rachel was the soft-spoken wife of a minister. "Yes, I did," came her answer, "but I'm not sure if it was just my own thinking or if it was really from God. But this is the picture I have in my mind. It's in Far Rockaway, on the left side of the tracks."

Jed thanked her and promised to pursue the lead.

Maybe while he had a bit of free time on Saturday

morning, he'd just take a quiet trip to Far Rockaway. If no one knew he had gone, no one would be disappointed if he failed. After all, the odds were wildly against him. It would be worse than a needle in a haystack. Far Rockaway, a tiny coastal town about twelve miles away, was only a handful of hay in the New York City stack. Furthermore, by now the van was surely stripped and burned.

Saturday morning brought clearer air and a merciful breeze, which helped to carry away some of the heat and smell. Jed slipped down the front steps and headed for his car, a block-and-a-half away. His courage wavered. Humanly speaking, the chances of finding the van were slim. How would he explain to Anton and Ralph where he had been all morning? He could hear himself answering their inquiry. "Uh, I was just out looking for the van."

And they'd probably ask, "In a city of eight million people or more? Are you crazy?"

As he unlocked his car, Kristie came up the sidewalk on her way to the drugstore. So much for slipping away unnoticed!

"Good morning, Jed. You're up and leaving early."

"Yes, I'm . . . well, I'm heading down to Far Rockaway. Guess I'll check out Sister Rachel's idea."

"Oh, good!"

"Actually, I was hoping to slip away without anyone knowing where I was going. I mean, it seems a little foolish to run down there on such abstract evidence."

Kristie smiled. "No, Jed, it's not abstract if God is behind it. I'll be praying that you find the van."

"Thanks, Kristie." With a wave, Jed jumped into his Geo Prizm and threw the "club" into the back seat. He prayed a short prayer and pulled away from the curb. Soon he was cruising along Rockaway Boulevard, heading for the southern edge of Long Island. When he turned off the boulevard and bumped across the railroad tracks, he felt a fresh wave of anxiety. *Just what will people say when I come back from this excursion with no van?*

The directions certainly weren't very specific. The left side of the tracks could mean anywhere from the tracks to the inlet. Jed decided to take the first street he came to and drive it slowly while scanning the vehicles parked along the curb. He turned right at the corner where there was an Irish store, then right again, heading back on a different street. Now and then he caught a glimpse of the beach between the houses.

Fifteen minutes into the search, Jed spotted a tan maxi van parked across from the subway stairs. It was identical to the book van except that it wasn't dark blue. Could it have been painted? Breathing faster, he slowed down. He saw a banana-size patch of rust along the wheel well. He shook his head and drove on—their van wasn't rusty.

Jed saw a number of other vans, including a blue one that made him gulp. But always something was missing or extra that didn't square with the van he'd driven just last Friday. Almost dizzy from looking back and forth, he decided to look for twenty more minutes. An hour of combing the town would be enough to convince him that the van was not there.

"Dear God," he prayed, "I can't stay here all weekend. You know where that van is, and You can help me find it if it's Your will. I know You can see the needle in the haystack, even if we can't."

The gas needle was dipping. Jed decided to find a gas station before he left town, if he could unwind himself from the tangle of one-way streets. He found Central Avenue and pulled into a Kwik Trip. There he filled his gas tank and grabbed breakfast—juice and bagel. It was actually closer to lunchtime, but he wasn't very hungry.

*Why did I come all the way out here?* Jed asked himself as he uncapped his juice. He steered into the right lane, heading out of town, and continued his thoughts. *Because it seemed the right thing to do, and maybe it still is the right thing.* He was ready to take a swallow when a patch of dark blue across the street jolted him.

*There is our van!* A chill went down his spine as Jed wheeled into the first available curb spot, half a block away. *Calm down,* he told himself, leaping out of his car and locking it with shaking hands. *Who says that's our van?* And yet he was sure. *There it is—the exact color, with tinted windows, chrome wheels—a little shinier than normal, maybe, but that would be expected if the thief intended to sell it.* Then his eyes fell on the last bit of clinching evidence. *There's the dent in the bumper on the driver's side—the dent Anton put in when he ran into a shopping cart rack at Wal-Mart. Now what shall I do next? I'll call Anton.*

Pulling out his cell phone, Jed dialed Anton's number. "Hello?"

"Anton, I'm in Far Rockaway, standing across the street from our van!"

"W-w-wait. This is Jed, isn't it? Back up and say that again."

"I came down to Far Rockaway to look for the van. It's a long story. I'll fill you in later. But I found it, and I think we need to move fast. It's our van—come down and help me bring it home!"

"You're sure it's our van?"

"As positive as I can be without checking the identification number. Bring the title and come down. Think I should call the police?"

"Better. Just hope no one drives off with it. Where'd you say you are?"

Jed gave him directions.

"I'm on my way. Sit tight and call me if anything happens."

Jed called the police and was told that an officer would be out within a half hour. As he slipped his phone back into his pocket, Jed suddenly felt very conspicuous. All this time, he had been standing on the sidewalk across from the van. Obviously, whoever put it there meant to come back for it, and that someone might not be an agreeable person to work with. But Jed was determined— *I'm not letting it out of my sight!*

Suddenly he felt ashamed. In his excitement, he had forgotten to thank God. With an overflowing heart, Jed poured forth praise and thanksgiving to his Lord.

Anton and the officer came within three minutes of each other. It was none too soon for Jed, who had been pacing the sidewalk, trying to look as ordinary as possible.

Anton spread out the title, and the officer studied it and took down the vehicle identification number. The thief had broken the lock, but Jed's key was a perfect fit. After checking with dispatch, the officer was convinced that Jed and Anton were in the right.

"It's your van, boys. Want me to call a wrecker to tow you home?"

"Sure, and thanks, officer," said Anton.

With a nod, the officer left.

"Is it just me," Jed asked, "or would it feel more comfortable to have him stay until the wrecker gets here?"

"I know what you mean. You think people are watching us?"

"Maybe we don't want to know. Did you get a good look in the van? Did they strip it?" asked Jed.

"Let's find out."

All the books and shelves were gone, and the steering column had been changed. But except for the broken lock, everything else was the same as before.

As Jed climbed out, he exclaimed, "Actually, I've never seen this van so clean. Just check out the wax job!"

"How about that!" Anton shook his head. "Now let's hear how you came down here. I still can't believe you found the van."

By the time the story was told, the tow truck arrived. After helping to load the van and giving the driver directions, the two young men drove safely away.

*Am I ever relieved to be out of there!* Jed felt weak as he thirstily drank his now-warm juice. It was afternoon. *I guess I should call someone.* He dialed Sister Rachel's number and got a busy signal. He tried Kristie next.

"Hello?"

"Kristie, this is Jed. We're coming home with the van."

"Oh, praise the Lord! Is it in good shape?"

"Missing the books and shelves, but all waxed up and 'clean as a whistle.' We're having it towed home."

"Oh, that's wonderful! Alas for the thief. I guess he didn't know what kind of God he was dealing with! I mean, looking for a car in New York City really is like looking for a needle in a haystack."

"Yes, it's definitely a miracle. I'm still in shock! We serve a *great* God."

Jed felt like smiling all the way home. As he followed the blue van through the largest city in the United States, he formed a new proverb. *It doesn't matter how big the haystack is if you have divine directions to the needle!*

# 57

## Bear One Another's Burdens

*Norma Plank*

In the early 1960s, my husband Marion Hartman and I were missionaries in Newfound, Kentucky. One time Loraine Bishop, one of our elderly members, was very ill—too ill for a 1½-hour jeep ride over very rough roads and creek beds. We had to travel some distance to a place with a telephone so we could call a doctor.

After Marion explained where Loraine lived, the doctor grudgingly agreed to come if someone would meet him at the swinging bridge and transport him to the Bishop home.

Marion explained that because our jeep was in a garage being repaired, we would have to take him in a trailer. It had bales of straw for seats and was pulled by our tractor. The doctor wasn't too happy, but agreed to meet us at a specified time.

While the doctor did not enjoy this adventure, our family did. When it was time to go to the bridge, we all piled in and sat on the bales of straw. When we got to the bridge, we saw the doctor's wife seated in the car. She had planned to sit there until the doctor returned, but we encouraged her to come along since there was plenty of room. We must have made it look like fun because she agreed. Later I'm sure she wished she had stayed in the car.

We were having a great time until we were nearly home and going down the last steep hill. Suddenly white fluid started squirting out in a great, pressurized arc every time the back wheel of the tractor went around. Now what? Marion speeded up and was able to park the tractor in the barn before the tire went completely flat.

Now our last means of transportation was disabled; we didn't even have a mule to take the doctor and his wife the three miles back to their car. To make matters worse, it was starting to rain. We invited the doctor's wife to come into our house while Marion and the doctor walked on to see a very sick Loraine. The doctor listened to her chest and said she had double pneumonia. He left some medicine but didn't tarry long, because darkness was coming early.

While the men were looking after the sick, I was feeling deep concern for the doctor's wife. She was in this predicament because we had insisted that she come with us in the trailer. It would be difficult to walk three miles in the rain over slippery, deeply rutted clay roads and ford several creeks. And besides, it was nearly dark.

Then the Lord spoke to me. *Give her your umbrella, your boots, and a high-powered flashlight.* Now those three things were very important to us in the rugged hills of Kentucky. We never knew when we would be called out into rain and mud to help someone at night. While I hesitated, the Lord reminded me, *Those articles can be picked up at the doctor's office in a few days when Marion takes your neighbors to town to shop.* I said, "Yes, Lord, I'm willing."

When I offered these articles, the doctor's wife hesitated until I assured her that my husband would be coming to town in a few days and would pick them up at the doctor's office. We had just slipped the boots over her shoes when Marion came in and said the doctor wasn't coming in; he was on his way out of the hollow. His wife grabbed the umbrella and flashlight and hurried after him. I felt sorry for her as I watched her husband striding ahead with angry steps. He neither looked back nor waited for her to catch up, but continued to lengthen the distance between them.

I have often wondered what happened during those three miles. If the lady fell, did her husband even find out and come to her aid? We never heard, but several days later Marion found the three items sitting in a corner of the doctor's waiting room, and he brought them home. I was happy to have those precious articles back, but I was also happy that I had listened to the Lord when He asked me to lend them to a woman in need.

# 58

## *Our Faithful Guide*

*Elizabeth Ann Shenk*

I was twenty-six when I married Raymond, a widower of fifty-four.

Before my marriage, I had taught school, helped mothers with new babies, and cared for invalids. My family didn't have a church home. I was earnestly seeking God's will for my life, but was not part of a church when my friendship with Raymond began. I did not know how to look to man for counsel. I only asked God.

God knew I wanted to know His will, and He also knew how sincerely I wanted to serve Him. So when I prayed for an answer from God about this unusual situation, the Lord spoke words into my mind. The words were separate from my normal thought processes.

The Lord said, "You will marry that man."

"But," I questioned, "I thought my life is to be a life of service."

"It will be a life of service," the Lord answered.

"But," I reasoned, "marriage is more than that."

"You will have a happy marriage," the Lord promised.

The Lord said no more. I had been taught not to trust in "visions and dreams," so I finished the prayer by saying, "Lord, if this is from You, You must show me." I did not tell Raymond about this until after we were married. I did not want to influence him. I knew he needed to hear from God himself.

I waited to see what would happen. At that time I was teaching school in Delaware, and Raymond lived in Maryland. He had many times of uncertainty, but six months into our friendship we had an unusual experience.

On the same day, we read Isaiah 55:8, 9 in our personal devotional time. "For my thoughts are not your thoughts, neither are your ways my ways, saith the LORD. For as the heavens are higher than the earth, so are my ways higher than your ways, and my thoughts than your thoughts." To Raymond, that was God's answer. To me, it was the confirmation of His words to me earlier. We were amazed during a phone conversation that we had both read the *same passage* on the *same day,* and that from it God assured *both of us* that our situation, though unusual, was His will. Two months later we married.

Then I shared with Raymond what God had told me at the beginning. Now, in 2007, we have been married twenty-five years, and I am the happy wife of a loving husband. God is *good.* He guides *faithfully.*

# 59

## *No Infirmities? No Glorying!*

*Elizabeth Ann Shenk*

Preparing to cut sweet potatoes to cook, I first sharpened a paring knife. As I began chunking the potatoes, the knife suddenly slipped and cut a deep slice into the little finger of my left hand. I wrapped a Band-aid tightly around the wound and finished the rest of the potatoes.

After putting them on to cook, I sat down to type a letter. Why would my little finger not bend to strike the keys? I was not pleased. That was my first clue that this was different from any other paring knife cut I'd ever had. My husband Raymond suggested I see a doctor.

The family doctor watched my inability to move my little finger and said, "You have severed the profundus tendon."

We thought he would stitch it up, and we'd be good to go. We were in for a surprise.

"You need to see a hand surgeon," the doctor said, and made an appointment for the next day.

Again, we expected the surgeon would stitch the tendon together and the problem would promptly be corrected. Not so.

"You need to go to the operating room and have the tendon repaired under anesthesia," he said. "After that, in order to successfully restore normal function, all the fingers of the left hand must be immobilized for up to eight weeks except for occupational therapy. Following that, for four more weeks there must be very little stress on that tendon."

We were stunned. I was even more displeased! All that for a cut on a little finger?

The surgeon explained, "If you had severed that tendon twenty years earlier, trying to restore normal function would not have been recommended, because such efforts were unsuccessful. But now, with improved techniques, function is largely restored—if everything is handled properly."

We chose to go ahead and let them try to help me. But I was upset that I needed to be disabled to that extent and for that length of time.

It reminded me of an ordeal I endured in July and August of 2005. I had had shoulder surgery, and for several weeks I couldn't use one arm. During that time I could not put up my own hair and was greatly inconvenienced in many other ways.

Now, resentment welled up as I thought of the inconvenience and the need of being dependent on the help of others again. I knew my attitude was wrong, so I asked God to help me understand the matter.

His answer came in the form of a question. "How can you glory in the things which concern your infirmities— if you have no infirmities?"

That was a rebuke and a challenge I needed to hear.

Through this experience, I learned to surrender to the rigors of looking at suffering as Paul did. "If I must needs glory, I will glory of the things which concern mine infirmities" (2 Corinthians 11:30).

# 60

## The Great Provider

*Norma Plank*

My husband Marion and I had been in service at the Lima City mission for four years when our home church asked us to serve at Wild Cat, Kentucky, where Merlin Good was minister. The church was already supporting two missionary families, and didn't feel they could support any more. So we were asked to try to support ourselves.

After much prayer, we notified the Lima City mission that we were leaving. A job running a carpenter shop had been found for Marion, so we agreed to go. We were in our twenties and had two little girls. Teresa was three, and Rita was eight months old. Little did we realize we were entering a wonderful learning experience and a daily walk by faith in God.

The people in the Wild Cat area were very poor, and few had money enough to ask Marion to make things for them in his shop, which was twelve miles away in Manchester. It was not unusual for us to have needs, but no money in our pockets. We didn't ask people to help us; rather, we learned to cry out to our heavenly Father, and He was always faithful. Because we didn't have a stable income, we never asked for credit. Instead, we paid cash or did without. We were surprised at how many things we really didn't need. Following are two examples of how God provided for us in a wonderful way.

\* \* \* \* \* \* \* \*

One evening, soon after Marion returned home from work, I mentioned that we had only enough milk to supply baby Viola for the following day. Marion would need to buy more on the way home from work the next day.

"Norma, I hate to tell you this," Marion said, "but I don't have one cent in my pocket. Also, I have enough gas in the car to take me to work in the morning, but not enough to bring me home."

While I was trying to digest that information, our little four-year-old Rita leaned her head against my side and whimpered, "I don't feel good."

I felt her head and discovered she was burning with fever. After putting her to bed on the living room couch, we applied home remedies to try to bring her fever down, but none seemed to help. Even if we took her to the doctor and asked for credit, there was not enough gas to bring us home. We prayed to God to heal our daughter. Finally she drifted off to sleep, and the next morning she awoke completely healed. How we praised God! Dry skin flaked off all over Rita's body from the high fever of the night before, but otherwise she was well.

After breakfast, Marion said, "Norma, what do you think I should do? Shall I go on to work and trust that God will send me some work? If He doesn't, I may need to stay in the shop all night, or until He does send work, so I can buy gas enough to get home."

After praying about it, we decided that God wanted Marion to stay at home until nine o'clock when the mail truck stopped at the little country post office, which was within sight of our house. We knew God could have laid it on someone's heart to send us some money. If He hadn't, Marion would go on to work and have faith that God would send him some work so he could provide for our needs. God had never failed us yet, and we were trusting in His promises.

We eagerly watched for the mail truck. As soon as it arrived, Marion hurried to the post office. He soon came striding back with two unopened letters.

We sat down in the living room, our eyes riveted on the letters. *What would the letters hold?* Marion opened the first and pulled out two handkerchiefs. I gasped. *Lord, are those handkerchiefs for us to wipe our tears?*

The next came from Lorene Shenk, my husband's cousin who lived in Florida. She could in no way have known of our desperate need, but the Lord had prompted her, days before we even realized our need, to send us five dollars. With gas selling for twenty-five cents per gallon, Marion would be able to fill up the car's gas tank and buy the milk and some other groceries—things we really needed. With our hearts overflowing, we joined hands in front of a blazing fireplace and sang the doxology—

> Praise God from whom all blessings flow,
> Praise Him, all creatures here below.
> Praise Him above, ye heavenly host;
> Praise Father, Son, and Holy Ghost!
> —Thomas Ken, 1695

This happened in the 1950s, but I still shed tears of joy in 2007, whenever that song is sung.

Marion went off to work with a happy, thankful heart. After filling the gas tank, he bought the needed groceries, and the total of all his purchases came to exactly five dollars. God is omniscient; we can fully trust Him to know just the amount we need.

\* \* \* \* \* \* \* \* \*

Another morning Marion said, "Norma, I still need twenty dollars to pay this month's bills—rent, lumber, and so on. I guess I shouldn't worry, because there are still three working days in this month, and likely God will send the needed work."

It so happened that people were coming from Elida, Ohio, to attend Hubert Sandlin and Waneta Brunk's wedding at Newfound. A number of friends stopped at our place on their way to the wedding.

Dale and Huldah Stemen were one couple who stopped, and Marion invited them in. Huldah came on

in, but Dale stood out by their car and visited with Marion.

After a while, Dale asked, "Marion, do you need some
money?"

Marion was not used to revealing our needs to anyone
but God, so he said, "That's a strange question, Dale.
Why do you ask?"

"Because," said Dale, "God told me to give this to
you." Then he pulled a twenty-dollar bill from his pocket
and shoved it into my husband's hand. Marion swallowed
a lump in his throat as he expressed his heartfelt thanks to
Dale and told him that was the exact amount we needed
to pay our bills that month.

Dale and Huldah soon left for Newfound. I'll never
forget the joy on Marion's face when he shared the good
news with me. Our wonderful Lord had met our needs
again.

# 61

## "Before They Call, I Will Answer"

*Evelyn B. Bear*

Midwestern blizzards are nothing to sneeze at, and this one was no exception. The wind was howling from the west, driving snow in almost horizontal lines across the countryside of northwestern Ohio. Schools were closed, farmers had battened down their barns full of animals, and all but the most necessary traffic had ceased. North-south roads were drifting more and more deeply. Staying inside was clearly the wisest thing to do.

Mark Bear, who had just entered his teens, was enjoying the unexpected day off from school. He especially welcomed one of his mother's home-cooked noon meals on a weekday. But during prayer before the meal, a nagging concern surfaced in Mark's mind. When the prayer was over, Mark asked his father, Paul, "Pop, I've been thinking about Grandpa Bear all morning. With this storm blowing, do you think somebody should go check on him?"

Paul looked intently at his son and replied, "I've been thinking the same thing. I think I'll call him first." After Paul ate, he crossed the room to the phone. He dialed his aging father's number and waited as the phone rang and rang and rang. Finally he replaced the receiver, turned to his family, and said, "He doesn't answer. That's not a good sign. I think I'd better go up there."

Paul's father Frank lived alone in his farmhouse about twenty miles north. Paul knew that to reach his father's home, he would be driving mostly on the badly drifted north-south roads, but he felt concerned enough that he didn't hesitate. He dressed in layers, warmed up his blue 1960 Chevrolet sedan, and headed north.

The going was slow, but Paul settled into a surging-slowing routine that allowed him to plow through most of the drifts. Sometimes he needed to stop, back up, and try again, but he always made it through until he reached the last intersection before his father's farm. Township trucks hadn't plowed that road yet, and it was drifted far too deeply for his car. He stopped to contemplate and to pray for wisdom.

Before long a snowplow pulled up beside him. Paul got the driver's attention and explained his dilemma. "No problem," said the driver. "Follow me, and I'll open 'er up for you." Thanking the Lord, Paul pulled in behind the snowplow, and slowly they made headway.

When Frank Bear's tall white farmhouse came into view through the blowing snow, Paul pulled as far into the driveway as he could manage. He waded through the deepening snow to the porch and knocked on the door. When there was no answer, he cautiously walked in.

No one was in the kitchen, so Paul continued into the dining room. There was his father, lying on the sofa and obviously not feeling well. "How are you doing, Pop?" was Paul's first question.

"Not too good, Paul."

"What's happened? Your fire is almost out, Pop," Paul noted. "It's getting cold in here."

Slowly, with great effort, Frank explained what had happened. He had gotten up at his usual time and started the fire. Then he prepared his breakfast and sat down at the kitchen table to eat. Suddenly he felt as if someone had "clubbed me to the floor," and that is where he found himself. He hadn't been able to get up; but finally he crawled into the dining room and managed to get onto the sofa, where he could lie down. That is where he had stayed until Paul found him.

Frank had suffered a stroke, and he was very weak and confused. In that condition, he hadn't even been able to think about praying for help. "Paul," he said, "I'm so glad you came. You know that verse 'Before they call, I will answer'? That's what happened today. You came even before I prayed."

Paul knew he needed to get his father into the car and seek medical help before the storm worsened. As he gathered up Frank's necessary belongings, shut down the stove, and prepared to close up the house, he mentally thanked the Lord over and over for the prompting that he and Mark had felt earlier that day. Had Paul not made that treacherous journey, his father might never have survived the coming night.

# 62

## *Vow! Plow! Wow!*

*Janet Good*

During his 1-W service my husband Richard Wenger was trained to be a respiratory therapist, which became a career and means of livelihood. After years of working in several hospitals in various communities, we planned to move to the Millersburg, Ohio area. An opening for a respiratory therapy supervisor became available at the hospital there, and Richard got the job. He was to start working on Wednesday, September 14, 1983.

Since our house hadn't sold yet in New Carlisle, Richard commuted the 150 miles to work. He left home on Tuesday, September 12, worked Wednesday through Friday and then returned home.

Richard returned to Millersburg on Sunday evening and worked Monday. At 4:00 p.m., Richard told a fellow therapist that he felt very tired, but he insisted on caring for his patients. He worked until midnight, and then went to the doctor's room where he had sleeping privileges.

The next morning the nurses heard a buzzing sound coming from Richard's room. At first they thought he was shaving, but when the buzzing continued, a nurse and an aid checked the room and found it was his alarm clock. And the Lord had taken Richard home.

The light was still on and the covers neatly pulled up. Apparently Richard had laid his Bible on the table beside the bed, and dropped his arm . . . and died. That's how they found him—dead of a heart attack. What a shock! But what a peaceful way to go! God had graciously waited until Richard went to bed to take him home.

After receiving the shocking news, the Lord impressed on my heart this message from Philippians 3:7-10: *What had been gain to me, I was to count as loss, that I may know Christ, the power of His resurrection, and fellowship of His sufferings.* The first night, Jesus put His arms around me and said, "I'll never leave you nor forsake you; I'll carry you through." It was so real and precious.

Arrangements were made to have Richard's funeral and burial at Sonlight Chapel near Apple Creek, Ohio, since that's where our family had planned to attend after we moved. On the day of the funeral someone said, "Janet, just remember God's grace will be there for you every day." I have often been encouraged by that thought.

* * * * * * * *

Our family and the family of Dave and Anna Good from Elida, Ohio, had been friends for years. We had visited in each other's homes. We had visited the Toledo

Zoo together. Our oldest children played together. The day of Richard's funeral, Dave kindly told my oldest son, Robert, "When you're ready, I want to use my truck to help you move." Dave moved us on January 1, 1984.

In the years following our two families were together occasionally. Dave and Anna attended my fiftieth birthday in October, 1993. Nine months later Anna had a brain aneurysm and was paralyzed on the left side. I saw them sometimes at the International Bible Fellowship Meetings in Indiana and at the Berean Meetings in Pennsylvania. In 2003 Anna went home to be with the Lord.

The following year my son Robert was visiting Mervin and Beverly Shirk in Elida. After church he told Merv he'd like to meet Dave Good, because he remembered our family times in the past.

This reminded Dave of Robert's mother, who had been a widow for more than twenty years. He remembered the good times our families had together thirty-five years earlier when we attended the same church. Six months later, after praying and seeking God's direction, he called me.

"Dave," I said, "I want to pray about it and counsel with my children. You may call back in two weeks."

My heart went out to the needs in Dave's family with two special sons—Steve with multiple sclerosis and Jim with schizophrenia. I also remembered the kindness and love Dave showed in caring for Anna while in a wheel chair for nearly ten years. I felt the Lord telling me this was His plan for me. "Thou wilt show me the path of life:

in thy presence is fulness of joy; at thy right hand there are pleasures forevermore" (Psalm 16:11).

Before Thanksgiving Dave called again and wondered if I was doing anything for Thanksgiving. He wondered if I would go with him to a wedding at the Sharon Church on Sunday morning for a seventy-nine-year-old widower and an eighty-year-old widow. I consented.

The following weekend we went to Lancaster, Pennsylvania to meet my parents. Dave proposed Saturday night. After my acceptance, we purposed in our hearts to always keep Jesus first in our lives.

We were married May 7, 2005. Brother John Brunk preached a message entitled, "Vow! Plow! Wow!" With a "Vow!" we look up to God and make our start together. To "Plow!" we look forward and do our part to have a happy union. And with a "Wow!" we look around with thankful hearts.

After a brief honeymoon, we concentrated on getting my house and things ready for an auction, which was scheduled for three weeks later. I needed to sort through things and decide what to keep and what to get rid of. We had a family auction, and the children got what they wanted.

For nearly a year before our wedding I would occasionally have severe headaches and have trouble keeping my balance. I had no headaches on the day of our wedding or on the honeymoon. But while preparing for the auction, the headaches and light-headedness came more frequently. We were sure it was stress.

The day of the auction I was not feeling well and did some strange things. After breakfast the children sent me to bed. When I got up, I passed out, and hit the corner of the dresser, cutting the top of my head. I must have lain there awhile before managing to get to the bathroom. My daughter Brenda found me, a bloody mess. She couldn't figure out what had happened.

Dave took me to Dr. Byler at Mt Eaton for five stitches. While we were gone, the children found blood on the carpet by the dresser; now they understood what had happened. Dave decided not to take me to the auction until the house was sold. When he took me over to sign the papers, I was hardly able to sign my name on the line.

My children and Dave decided I should be taken to the hospital. My symptoms reminded Dave of Anna before her aneurysm. A CAT scan was done about 10:00 p.m. An hour later Dave was still waiting for a report. He began thinking something must be very wrong. Finally just before midnight a very sober doctor came in. "Janet has a tumor on her brain, but our hospital is not equipped to care for her problem."

I was taken by ambulance to the St. Rita's Medical Center in Lima, Ohio, which was close to where Dave and I were living.

Dave needed to call the family, but first he needed some time alone. He didn't want to break down in front of me, so he went outside the hospital and cried out to God. "Lord, this is so hard, but I want to accept whatever

You have planned for us. I hate to tell Jim and Steve such news. They were so happy to have a mother again, and now here she is in the hospital with a brain tumor. You, alone, can give us the strength we need at this time."

When the neurosurgeon in Lima looked at the CAT scan Saturday morning, he said, "It's too large a tumor to operate on. It looks like it has fingers."

As I thought about what Dave had gone through with Anna, and now with me, just four weeks after we were married, I said, "Lord, must Dave go through this again?"

"I hope you didn't get a lemon," I told Dave.

He assured me that he would love me no matter what.

Then the Lord reminded me of the passage in James 5. "Is any sick among you? Let him call for the elders of the church, and let them pray over him, anointing him with oil in the name of the Lord." I felt God wanted me to take that step, so Dave made arrangements with his bishop, John Brunk, and my bishop, Ray Shaum. Many prayers went up for us all over the U.S. and elsewhere.

Dave said, "It looks like God has some more "plowing" for us to do." He was remembering our wedding sermon—
*Vow! Plow! Wow!*

On Sunday morning, eight of our ten children and their companions were in my Intensive Care room singing. "Our God, He Is Alive," "Each Step I Take," "Does Jesus Care?" and "What a Friend We Have in Jesus," rang through the room.

I asked a nurse if we were too loud.

She said, "Oh, no, I'm benefiting too."

On Monday morning I had an MRI. At 9:00 a.m. John Brunk and Ray Shaum led a very meaningful anointing service. We felt the presence of the Lord. Again we sang and prayed.

At noon I was scheduled for a biopsy. Before I was wheeled into the operating room, a nurse said she would be with me and wanted to pray. She prayed a powerful prayer for my healing—recognizing our great Creator, Saviour, and Healer.

On Wednesday morning, Dr. Lax came into my room. "I got the results of the biopsy late Tuesday night," he said. "After studying it, I found the tumor is smaller than I first thought—about the size of a tangerine. I believe the finger-like appearance was probably due to swelling. The tumor is benign. It's on the right side—the best side and the best kind—that is, if you are going to have a tumor. I'm scheduling you for surgery on Thursday morning, and I think I can get ninety-five percent of it. Let me know what your decision is."

Dave and I prayed and felt led to go ahead with surgery.

As I was wheeled into the operating room, the nurse who had prayed for me on Monday showed me a piece of paper with Psalm 40:1 written on it: "I waited patiently for the LORD; and he inclined unto me, and heard my cry."

She said, "The Lord is going to heal you."

After surgery, Dr. Lax told Dave and the family that I came through very well, and he had gotten 100% of the tumor. Oh, glory! What marvelous news! Later, we thanked Dr. Lax for what he had done, but we also wanted God to be praised, so we told him thousands of people had been praying for him during my surgery. He just smiled.

We felt the power of prayer and strength from the Lord and a freedom in the hospital to exalt His Name. Dave stayed with me day and night.

Three days after surgery I was released.

One morning after I was home, Dave and I read Psalm 46. We especially commented on verses one and ten. "God is our refuge and strength, a very present help in trouble."

We had vowed, and plowed, and now we had experienced the "Wow!" of Brother John Brunk's message. We marveled at how God showed Himself strong and gave us this opportunity to exalt Him. We continue to thank God for His goodness in answering prayers for healing and for continuing to give us a joyful journey together.

# VI.

GOD SPEAKS THROUGH STRONG

*Promptings*

# 63

## The Faith of a Little Child

*Norma Plank*

My husband and I were moving to Newfound, Kentucky, to serve as missionaries, along with our five children aged three to ten years old. The area was very rough in more ways than one. Our car could go no closer than 3½ miles to our house, but our church would furnish us with a four-wheel-drive jeep.

Very early on our moving day, Clarence Bear, one of our church brethren, started out in his tarp-covered stake truck loaded with our furniture. He started before we did, but we hoped to overtake him and arrive first, so we could tell the men where to set the furniture when they unloaded. The last nine miles were over a very narrow road of mud and rock, and there would be no way to pass the truck. We also knew the truck could only inch its way along while trying to protect the vehicle and our furniture from too much damage. It might take three hours instead of the usual 1½ hours to travel those nine miles.

Rudy Brunk, the former missionary, met us with the church jeep as planned and showed us where to park our car. Since we had not caught up with our load of furniture, we had two choices: either take a shortcut by fording the river, or creep along behind the slow-moving truck.

"I hear there has been heavy rain up the river," Rudy said, "but there's a chance that we can still ford the river if the water isn't too high."

We had given up all hope of passing our load of furniture, so we decided to take a look at the river. Shifting the jeep into the lowest gear possible, we crept down a very steep trail running parallel to the river. Finally we were down at the level of the water. We sat there awhile trying to decide whether we should try to cross the rising river.

Finally Rudy said, "I believe we can make it, but be sure to stay up close to the ripples."

My husband was driving while Rudy gave directions. Soon after entering the water, the tailpipe on the jeep was submerged, and we could hear the exhaust going *blub, blub, blub* like a motorboat. We angled upriver to the ripples and followed along beside them. The water became deeper and deeper until it started coming into the jeep.

"This has never happened before," Rudy said uneasily.

Soon we were holding our feet above five inches of water! We were a little past the middle of the river when our motor flooded and stopped. The current was swift, and the jeep was shuddering as if it could roll any minute—and none of us knew how to swim. We didn't know what to do. Our children realized that we were in real danger.

Our three-year-old Delbert reached up and patted my shoulder. "Mommy, can't we pray about it?" he said in a frightened voice.

"Sure," I reassured him. "We can pray about it."

Daddy prayed a short-and-to-the-point prayer, but during that prayer, God put a thought into my head that He alone could have put there. I'm no mechanic, so I know it was His thought, not mine.

When the prayer was over I said, "I just had a thought. Is it possible to put the jeep in the lowest gear, hold the ignition key on, and run the jeep out of the river just on the strength of the battery?"

"I don't know," my husband said. "I really doubt if the battery is strong enough to pull us out of the river. But it won't hurt to try, and I don't have any better idea."

He shifted into low, and then, while the rest of us held our breaths, he turned the key. The starter caused the motor to turn over, which made the wheels turn slowly. As the motor labored, we heard a slow *chug-a, chug-a, chug-a* as the wheels clambered over the river rocks. Very slowly we crept across the river. *Would the battery hold out?*

Finally the water started running out from the jeep floor. Hurrah! We knew we had reached shallower water. When we were nearly to the other side and no longer in danger of being rolled over by the rushing water, my husband stopped holding the key. Opening his door, he swung his leg out over the top of the door, and crawled out onto the fender. Then he unlatched and folded back the noisy metal hood from the side. I winced as I saw him pull out his nice, clean, white hanky and use it to dry off the spark plugs and distributor—or whatever you dry off on a motor.

After he had latched the clattery hood, my husband climbed back into the jeep. We were all wondering, *Would the jeep start? Had we run the battery too low?* We all listened with bated breath as he turned the key. Sure enough, the motor sprang to life! Soon we *blub, blub, blubbed* our way out of the river.

I don't remember who started a praise song, but someone did, and all of us joined in as we bounced our way up a steep, rocky hill. I've never experienced a more inspirational praise service as we rocked and bumped our way over those horrible roads. We sang one praise song after another until we reached our new home. We even arrived before the truck with our furniture.

For nearly fifty years, I've remembered that precious moving-day experience, and I'm still praising God for it. He had given us guidance from Heaven, spared our lives, and increased our faith. Do you think I believe that God speaks to His children today? Yes, without a doubt!

# 64

## "No, Don't Come In"

*Chester Heatwole*
*As told to Norma Plank*

Wilmer lived in the Peake community with his sister. I don't think Wilmer was ever married. He suffered a lot physically as a result of drinking and other bad habits. Because of his ailments Wilmer spent a lot of time in bed.

Once I stopped by to visit them, and the sister came to the door alone. "Come in," she said. "I'm glad you're here. My brother isn't feeling well, and I wish you would visit him. He's in his room." She motioned down the hall.

I went down the little hall to his bedroom and knocked on the door. I heard a man's voice, but couldn't understand what he said. I said who I was, and that I wanted to talk to him. "May I come in?" I asked.

"No!" he said, "I don't want you to come in."

"But, I want to come in and talk to you."

Again he said, "No!"

It's not that I'm a great conversationalist, but I wanted to talk to Wilmer. And I knew why he didn't want to talk to me. I felt the Lord prompting me to talk to this man, so I continued talking as I slowly opened the door. That wasn't very smart, but I felt God was leading me. I peeked into the room. It was so dark I couldn't tell anyone was there.

As I continued talking, I could tell Wilmer wasn't minding too much after all. I talked to him about the Lord Jesus, the great Shepherd of the sheep and the Saviour to the world. When we finished our conversation, Wilmer wanted to receive Jesus as his Saviour, and gave his heart to the Lord.

After his conversion, the way was opened for more visits. I visited Wilmer many, many times—in the very room I had been told not to enter. Now Wilmer wanted me to come in.

I was very glad I had obeyed the voice of the Lord telling me to speak to Wilmer. John 3:16 says, "For God so loved the world, that he gave his only begotten Son, that whosoever believeth in him should not perish, but have everlasting life." It was a great blessing to see Wilmer be included in "whosoever" as he embraced God's loving call to salvation.

## Eternity – One Step Away

Chester Heatwole
*As told to Norma Plank*

Harold Shoemaker lived in the Peake community. Likely in his fifties, he was not a Christian and made no room for church in his life. Harold cut and sold wood to make a living, and he worked hard.

Whenever we met, I made it a point to talk to him. During our revival meetings, evangelist Ivan Weaver and I decided to invite Harold to the meetings.

We caught Harold at home one evening. Sometimes such fellows leave when they see the preacher coming, but he stayed and we sat in the living room and talked. We told him about our revivals, and that he was totally welcome to attend. In fact, we would be excited to see him come.

The conversation continued—sometimes about spiritual things, and sometimes earthly. Harold was in a talkative mood. His wife sat quietly, listening. She had grown up Mormon, a background quite different from Mennonites.

Finally, I thought it was time for us to leave. We had walked to the front door when suddenly I felt a strong urge from the Lord to talk to Harold a little more. I turned and went back to him, still seated in his chair.

I pleaded with the man. "Harold," I said, "wouldn't you like to be a Christian?"

"Yes!" he said.

His response took me off guard; I think my face showed my surprise.

"I'm very happy to know this," I exclaimed. "Would you like to become a Christian right now?"

"Yes!" he repeated.

So the Spirit led, and Harold came to know the Lord, confessing Christ as his personal Saviour.

As we continued talking, he told me about a heart problem he had. However, he explained that he had gone to the hospital and it was all fixed up.

"I'm better than I ever was," Harold said. "I should live for many years."

The evangelist and I left the house, rejoicing that another soul had found peace with his Maker.

Within two hours we received a shocking phone call that Harold had suddenly dropped over dead!

This news shook the community, and the Lord really spoke to us all. It shook his Mormon wife to the point that she wanted the Mennonites to have the entire funeral service. I was so glad that Harold had found the Lord. To think—he was just one step away from being eternally separated from God.

I have thought about this many times. Suppose I hadn't gone back and talked to him when the Lord urged me? It should be a valuable lesson to all of us. Let us be faithful and heed the Lord's promptings, even if it means returning to someone and resuming our witness effort for Christ.

# *Lasting Regrets*

*Norma Plank*

A deadly feud had gone on for years between the White and Webb families. They took turns killing—one from the Webb clan would be murdered, and then one from the White clan. In 1955 it was the year for one of the Webbs to die. The police knew about the problem but refused to get involved.

The Webbs lived back in one of the Kentucky hollows and worked hard on their bottomland farm. Mr. and Mrs. Webb and their two sons and two daughters lived in constant fear. When darkness fell in the evening, they hung covers over every window before lighting a lamp. The doors and windows were locked—winter and summer. The father seemed to know he was the next target, because he always had two large revolvers hanging in leather holsters, one on each hip.

Eventually the family built a nice house on a hill across the road from our place and moved out of the hollow. Mr. Webb, with his heavy revolvers flopping at his side, would walk across our property when he returned to his farm in the hollow. He would only grunt in response to our greetings. He never smiled. God had laid a heavy burden on my heart for this man's soul.

One day after my husband had gone to work, a noise caused me to look out our living room window. A missionary from another mission station had stopped at our front gate. Just as he was getting out of his car, I saw Mr. Webb coming back from his farm. He would soon walk right past the missionary.

The Lord told me, "Go out there and ask Mr. Webb if all is well with his soul."

I argued, "But Lord, I'm a woman, and there is a missionary man out there. Get him to do it."

When the missionary came into our house, I asked, "Did you ask Mr. Webb about his soul's need?"

"No, I didn't," came his ready reply. "I never met the man before, and when I saw those two revolvers, I thought I'd better tread softly."

How I wished I had obeyed the Lord's bidding! I had a heavy feeling that something terrible was about to happen.

The very next day we heard the tragic news. Mr. Webb was driving his small tractor, with his teenage daughter riding behind him, when he was ambushed. Three shots were fired, striking his head, chest, and stomach. Mr. Webb was dead; he had no more opportunity to prepare to meet his Maker.

I can't begin to tell you the grief I endured. Why had I argued with God? Now I could see clearly how well the

Lord had everything worked out to the minute. The Lord caused the missionary to stop just as Mr. Webb walked by; and because I was acquainted with the man, God had asked me to do a very simple thing—just ask him if all was well with his soul. If he had showed signs of wanting help, there was the missionary man to talk with him.

Regret and tears are hard things to live with. It is now over fifty years later, and I can hardly talk about this incident without tears. The Lord taught me that day the importance of being swift to obey the Spirit's promptings. We may not have a second chance.

Our family attended Mr. Webb's funeral and burial, which took place right in the yard at their new house. Such weeping and wailing I had never witnessed.

A neighbor told us later that she saw Mrs. Webb put her hand on the shoulder of her twelve-year-old boy. "Son," she said, "it will now be your responsibility to kill one of the Whites."

We moved away soon after that happening, but I often wondered if the Prince of Peace was ever invited into that home. He would have been well able to stop the terrible feud that had been controlling their lives for many years.

# 67

## *Mother's Great God*

*Martha Martin*

As many people know, it is when our burdens are extremely heavy that we experience God's personal presence drawing very near. My mother found this to be true in her life. She is no longer here to tell her story, so I will tell it.

Daddy had been in a serious accident—so serious that he wasn't expected to live. This is how it happened. One evening after dark he was hauling a tractor to our farm on the back of a truck. Along the way he stopped by the road to see if the chains that held the tractor in place on the truck bed were still snug. But first he checked to make sure all the truck lights were visible.

Just then an elderly man came along. Blinded by the lights of an oncoming car, he didn't see Daddy standing at the rear of the truck and crashed into him, pinning him underneath the truck.

At the hospital Daddy was thoroughly examined. The doctors inserted pins into his legs and put him in traction, which held his legs by pulleys and weights. Three weeks later, he had no feeling in his severely mangled right leg, and the leg had to be amputated above the knee.

Mother had to be strong—driving back and forth to the hospital to care for her husband, plus looking after her five children (ages five to twelve) at home. Adding to the physical and psychological stresses were financial pressures. Mother's single sister came to live with us for a while. She and Mother made our dresses and slips out of feed bags. Money was so tight that Mother had to borrow ten cents from Aunt Betty to purchase buttons and snaps for the dresses.

Daddy spent eight weeks in the hospital, six weeks at home in a body cast from his chest to his toes, and then about six more weeks in the hospital. By that time he was very weak and had to learn to walk all over again—this time with an artificial leg. A frame made of pipes gave him peripheral support, with a seat attached at one corner for him to sit on when he became tired. He learned to do many new things, like driving a car with hand controls and going down steps backward instead of forward.

When Daddy returned home and could mostly care for himself, Mother got a job sewing children's snowsuits at a sewing factory in town. She would get up at 3:00 a.m. on washdays and do the family laundry before going to work. After work she would help milk the cows by hand and do other farm chores.

At one point the load seemed so heavy that Mother felt she couldn't take any more. That's when God seemed very near; she felt an arm go around her shoulders. When she turned to see who was there, she was alone—all by herself, except for her heavenly Father.

For about nineteen more years Daddy lived a fairly normal life because of his stamina, determination, and trust in God. But at the age of fifty-two, he had a massive heart attack and died in his sleep.

Again a heavy burden fell on Mother. At the time, I was engaged and would soon be married to Willard Martin. I remember telling Mother that I didn't think I could give up my loved one as submissively as she gave up Daddy. She replied, "Oh, yes, you could. But God doesn't give us grace until we need it." It was obvious that He was giving grace to Mother as she needed it.

As a result of Daddy's accident and the nursing care Mother needed to give him, she became interested in nurse's training. The youngest of her children, I was in high school when Mother got her LPN degree. She served others as a nurse for many years.

Mother had a strong trust in God and was submissive to His will, but there were still many decisions to make. Some of these were very difficult, and she often struggled with loneliness. At one particularly stressful time she prayed, "Lord, help me. I just don't know what to do."

An audible voice told her, "John Hershey will help you."

Mother replied, "Oh, no, Lord; I didn't mean something like that!"

But in time John Hershey did help her by marrying her, with the blessing of both her children and his. They had five happy years together, and then he also died of a heart attack. Mother had the difficult experience of seeing both of her husbands die suddenly right in her presence.

Mother passed away on April 3, 2004, still clinging to the Lord and quoting Scripture as she was dying. She has often been an inspiration to me.

# Obedient to God's Purposes

*The story of a man who worked with the underground church*
*Norma Plank*
*Rewritten by permission*

I was asked to meet with a group of eight leaders of the North Korean underground church. As I entered a small room, I noticed an old man sitting in a corner. We started talking about the underground church situation and ways believers survived during severe persecution.

Abruptly, one of the young leaders turned to me and said, "Teacher." He paused and took a deep breath, and then continued, "We would like to escape from North Korea. Would you help us?"

I was taken aback. "How many leaders want to leave the country?" I asked.

"Eighty," he replied.

I began calculating the cost. *Arranging for eighty people to secretly escape from North Korea into a friendly country will take between 250,000 and 500,000 dollars. This is no small amount for our humble ministry. But their lives are worth so much more, even if I need to get a second mortgage on my house or sell it outright.*

When I concluded my calculations, I stood and said, "When shall we do it?"

The leaders' faces beamed with gratitude at my decision.

Then the old man who had been sitting quietly all this time, stood slowly and said, "Teacher." (He was much older than I, yet he humbly called me teacher.) "May I pray to God about this once more?"

"Certainly," I replied.

As he moved into the adjoining room, we all thought he would spend two or three hours talking with God. We were surprised when he returned very soon, looking confident. We waited expectantly.

"What did God say?" I gently prompted.

"God said . . ." he paused and then continued, "that we should not go. He told me we should stay in North Korea. He even asked whether I thought He was powerless to care for us here." The old pastor went on, "God also said, 'I could move all of you out of North Korea instantly, but I have a purpose for which I desire you to stay.'"

The old leader said he was surprised to learn that God was in their suffering and that it all had a purpose. He asked God if it was His will that they were starving in North Korea, and God had answered, "Yes."

"Is it also Your will for us to be beaten up?" asked the old man. "Is it Your will for us to go to jail and die?"

God had replied, "Of course."

The old leader's eyes were brimming with tears. "I finally realized that God has a purpose for allowing His people to be persecuted," he said.

Then he looked at me and said, "Teacher, I am so sorry to have troubled you to come this far, and to now tell you that we cannot leave. God wants us to pour out our lives to tend His church in North Korea."

Holding back the tears, he continued, "Please return home. Teacher, you have done much for us, and we are comforted because we know there are many who pray for us outside in other countries. Tell them God wants us to remain in North Korea and to keep our faith until the very end."

With tears streaming down his face, he added, "Though I want to have freedom, I will obey my God. This is what He wants." His face changed, and he spoke boldly. "We will follow His will and stay for His church."

As one, the seven other leaders nodded their heads in agreement. Regardless of the cost, they also would obey.

The old man turned to me. "Now go! Quickly!" he said firmly. He did not want anyone's resolve to weaken, so he was chasing me out. But I couldn't help it; we held each other and cried together for a time.

As I prepared to leave, those eight brave men held hands and began to pray, "We thank You, O Lord. You have given us Your clear word; You have a purpose for us to stay in North Korea. Although we are persecuted, we will worship You."

As I left the meeting, I was convinced that God is preparing to do something great. He is strengthening and restoring His church in North Korea.

This past year, God spoke His heart to our ministry. He said, "Recapture Pyongyang."

Pyongyang, North Korea's capital, once burned with revival fires to the point that it was called the "Jerusalem of the Orient." Those embers are beginning to glow brightly as the Holy Spirit fans them back into flame once again.

For the past nineteen years, we have faithfully delivered Bibles into North Korea, and God has told us to advance upon Pyongyang. This we will do in the strength of the Lord. Our job is to pray and encourage the underground churches in North Korea, but we know that any revival there will not come in from the outside. It will spring into flame from the blood of the martyrs, from the hearts of faithful underground leaders, like those eighty who are willing to take up the cross and pour out their very lives as a fragrant offering to the Lord. It will also come through the powerful witness of the Holy Spirit working marvelous signs and wonders.

# The Roaring Lion, Second in Power

*Norma Plank*

Clint looked lovingly at his wife. "We had some very rough sledding in our marriage before we were Christians," he said. "I'm sorry about that, Darlene, but we've also had some rough times since our conversion. We have so much to learn about the Christian life. I'm just thankful for the pastor and his wife and for the brothers and sisters in the church who have encouraged us."

Clint paused a moment and then asked, "Are your sisters still giving you a hard time?"

"They tell me I'm losing my mind; that I'm stupid and crazy. They also think I'm crazy to continue living with you. But Mum encourages me to stay with the church we're with, because she can see that you and I are happier than we've ever been before."

"You have a very dear mother, Darlene. I can't complain about her. She treats me like a son. I wish your sisters were more understanding."

"Their comments are painful. They call my veiling a gravy strainer or a goldfish net. They say I look ugly without my hair dyed and wearing my conservative dress." Darlene's voice quavered. "And my closest sister refuses to speak to me. I'm never to call her on the phone. It hurts, Clint."

"I'm sure it does, because you and your sisters were very close. I never experienced such closeness in my family. Darlene, I want you to know something: you look beautiful to me in your plain dress and veil. You do have friends. It's easy to see that the women at church really love you."

"Yes, the sisters in our church are dearer than my own flesh and blood. I thank God for them," said Darlene with a sigh. "And I can say I'm happier than I've ever been. I never knew you could be so nice to live with. You know, Clint, after we were married, I used to tolerate you, but now I love you. You're so different. It's like we're on our honeymoon. I'd never want to go back to our old life."

"Nor I. I agree with all my heart. It's wonderful to enjoy one another and not just tolerate each other."

Two days later, Clint and his family walked into Lighthouse Mennonite Church. The congregation met in a community center. An inspirational Sunday school and preaching was followed by a wonderful time of fellowship.

Darlene said to one of the other women, "You know, in the other church we attended, only a few people might shake your hand and then quickly walk outside and leave. I enjoy the warm fellowship here."

When Darlene saw Clint was ready to leave, she explained to her friend, "We're having lunch with my mother, and we're taking the meal."

"I hope you have a good visit, Darlene. We'll see you at the evening service," said her friend.

"We'll be here," replied Clint and Darlene together.

* * * * * * * *

The family had a good visit with Darlene's mother, whom the grandchildren called "Nanny." Clint always felt at home in his mother-in-law's apartment. He lay on the couch in her spare room and took a nap.

That evening, the family went to church again. At the close, the leader said, "Brother Clint, please lead us in the closing benediction. Let us stand."

The congregation stood to their feet and Clint began, "We thank You, heavenly Father, for this wonderful day of worship. We pray that we will all stay true and faithful to You throughout this coming week. Just keep us from the evil one, who, like a roaring lion, is going about seeking to devour us. In Jesus' name, Amen."

On Monday, Clint stayed home because he didn't have any carpenter work lined up. Darlene's mother called in the afternoon. "I can't find my wallet," she said.

"That's too bad, Mum. Why don't you ask your pastor if it's on any of the church pews or in the parking lot at your church. You might also look in your coat pocket."

"Darlene," said her mother quietly, "your sisters and I have torn this house apart looking everywhere, and it's nowhere to be found."

"Well, Mum, what do you all think might have happened to your wallet?" asked Darlene.

"Darlene, my purse was in the spare room, and your sisters know that Clint and your children were the only ones in there yesterday. I don't care about the 150 dollars in my wallet; it's the many cards I use for buying, banking, and health care that I hate to lose."

Darlene was shocked. "Mum!" she cried, "I know my children would never steal from you. They love you. Clint does too, and I know he wouldn't steal from you either."

"I don't like to think of the possibility either, Darlene, but where is my wallet?"

Darlene suggested several other places where her mother could look, and then she hung up the phone. Clint looked at her with concern and asked, "What was that all about?"

"My mother can't find her wallet, and my sisters are blaming you or our children for stealing it. They say you were the only ones in the spare room where she keeps her purse."

The accusation pierced Clint's heart like a dagger. *I would never steal from my mother-in-law. She's been more of a mother to me than my own mother has. Those sisters hate us; they want to spoil our Christian home, that's what.*

Suddenly his temper exploded, and Clint forgot he was a child of the King. Vile words spewed out of his mouth—words he had often used before he was born again. "I didn't do it!" he shouted. "Tell me you don't believe I could do such a thing, Darlene," Clint demanded.

In a quiet voice Darlene said, "Clint, I'm not accusing you. But I am doubting you because of the way you're acting—exploding like that. You're acting guilty."

Clint's temper was still in high gear. "If you don't trust me, I don't see how this family can stay together!" he shouted. "I'll sleep in Shi-Enne's bed tonight, and she can sleep with you." With that Clint stomped up the stairs.

Darlene gathered their children close and said, "We'll go ahead with the Bible reading as usual. Let's sing the songs your father likes best, and then have prayer." Darlene thought, *Clint loves to sing. Maybe when he hears us singing his favorite songs, he'll join us. I hope so.*

* * * * * * * *

Clint entered his little girl's room and threw himself across the bed, his anger still boiling. Suddenly he found himself listening keenly. Was that Darlene leading out in family worship? He groaned. *They probably don't even miss me. They know I'm supposed to be the one to lead out in such things. Nobody trusts me—not even Darlene. What's the use?*

Clint groaned again when he heard them singing his favorite songs. He turned up some music to cover the sounds from downstairs. There followed a whole night of tossing and turning; Clint found no escape in sleep. He was miserable. Would the night never end so he could leave the house?

The next morning he heard the family eating breakfast and again reading from the devotional book and Bible. He could hardly keep the sobs back as the singing floated up the stairs. When the children were ready for school, Clint came down and sat in the car, his face haggard.

The children came out and silently got into the car with him. It was the quietest ride they'd had in a long time—even little Shi-Enne had nothing to say, though she cast loving glances at her father. When she got out of the car, she said, "I love you, Dad."

Clint gulped, trying to swallow the lump in his throat. "I love you too," he murmured with a heavy sigh, hardly trusting his voice.

Clint drove to where he was working. Though he was weary, he forced himself to clear snow out of the driveway. Soon Ken, a brother in the church, came to work with him.

Miserable and dejected, Clint raised his eyes to Ken. "Brother Ken, may I share a burden that's heavy on my heart?" Clint dropped onto an overturned bucket, his head hanging in defeat.

Ken gently placed his hand on Clint's shoulder and said, "Yes, please tell me about it."

Clint brokenly told the whole miserable story. Then he said, "My family thinks I'm guilty, and Darlene's sisters are persuading my dear mother-in-law to believe I am too. What shall I do?"

"Listen, Clint," said Ken. "I want you to know I do not believe you took that wallet. I trust you. Now, about your next step—you said you lost your temper last night, used some bad language, and said some cutting things to Darlene. Your children were there and heard it all. What do you think you should do about that?"

"I need to ask their forgiveness, and I'll do that the first chance I get. Thank you, Brother Ken, for listening to me and for having faith in me. I'm beginning to feel better already." Clint wiped his eyes.

Clint's cell phone rang. It was Darlene. "Listen, Clint, Mum says that my sister is planning to take her purse to the police station and get it fingerprinted."

"Thanks for telling me, Darlene. And I'm terribly sorry for the way I acted last night. I was very hurt, but that was no excuse for my conduct. I'll be home tonight and confess my wrongs to you and the children.

"That sounds like my Clint. I'll be waiting for you," encouraged Darlene.

Clint shared the conversation with Ken. Then they had prayer about the threat to have the purse fingerprinted.

When they finished, Clint made a sudden decision. "You know, Ken, I'm anxious to have this thing settled. I didn't take the wallet, so I'm going down to the Royal Canadian Mounted Police station and ask them to take my fingerprints. Then when Darlene's sister brings the purse in, the proof will already be there."

He drove away and was soon at the station. Clint explained the whole story to the policeman on duty.

"I've heard a lot of things, but I've never had anyone come in and want their fingerprints taken ahead of time. I can't do what you asked, though, because you're not charged with a crime. The way I see it, you don't have much to worry about. If you were guilty, you wouldn't have come in. Just go home and relax," said the officer.

Clint went to the car and called his wife. "Darlene, I'm at the police station. I tried to get him to take my fingerprints so that . . . "

"You what? You wanted them to take your fingerprints? Why would you do a thing like that?" quizzed an excited Darlene.

"I wanted to make it easy for your sister when she brought the purse down. I want this problem settled the quickest way possible. Since your sister won't allow you to call her, just tell your mum to tell her to be sure to talk to Officer O'Ryan. He knows the whole story."

"Oh, Clint, if you've done all that, I'm convinced you're not guilty. Never once did I tell my mother or my sisters that I doubted you. You and our children are the only ones who know that. I'm so sorry I doubted you. Will you forgive me?"

"Yes, with all my heart. Your trust means so much to me, Darlene," Clint said, his voice breaking.

After laying down the phone, he bowed his head. "Lord, please forgive me for losing my temper and saying such vile words. I was such a poor example to my children and I hurt Darlene too, just when things were going so well between us," Clint said tearfully. "Please, Lord, let that wallet be found. You know exactly where it is, and I know You will reveal it in your time. I refuse to worry about it any longer, because I'm trusting You to work it all out."

When Clint opened his eyes, the future looked bright again. God had spoken peace to his heart and had assured him the wallet would be found. *I may as well go home,* he thought. *The workday is nearly over, and I'm anxious to get things straightened out with my family. Oh, Lord, I realize how weak I am and how much I need You. Help me as I confess my sins to my children, and give them the strength they need to have forgiving hearts.*

\* \* \* \* \* \* \* \*

Darlene shook her head as she turned away from the phone. *What a man!* she thought. *How he must have suffered! Forgive me, Lord, for doubting my husband and helping to put the same doubts in our children's minds. Set a guard at my lips, dear Lord.*

Darlene picked up the phone and called her mother. "Mum, Clint went to the police station and asked them to take his fingerprints so that when my sister brings in the purse, this problem can be quickly solved. The policeman said he couldn't take any fingerprints until Clint is charged. Will you please tell my sister that? Tell her to speak to Officer O'Ryan, because he knows the whole story."

Her mother said, "Oh, Darlene, I don't want to file charges against Clint. Let's just forget the whole thing."

"But Mum, don't you see—Clint needs his name cleared. He's hurting. His children need to know their father is not guilty. I'm sure you understand that."

"Darlene, I don't know what to think," said her mother.

"Well," urged Darlene, "please send your purse down to the station for fingerprints, so Clint's good name can be restored."

Before they hung up the phone, her mother agreed to think about it.

\* \* \* \* \* \* \* \*

Clint called his mother-in-law and asked, "Mum, did you find your wallet yet?"

"No, Clint," she answered, "We've looked everywhere, and it has not been found. I always return my wallet to the inside compartment in my purse, and I always pull the zipper shut. When I went to get my wallet, the side zipper was open and the wallet was gone. It looks like theft."

"Yes," agreed Clint, "it does look that way, but please believe me. I did not take it. We are praying, and God has given me the assurance that your wallet will be found."

When the conversation ended, he bowed his head and silently prayed, *Thank You, Lord, for giving me the grace to call Darlene's mum. Help her believe that I am innocent.*

As soon as Clint arrived home, he told each of his children how sorry he was for the way he had talked and acted the night before. They readily forgave him. Then he said to them all, "I've asked the Lord to forgive me, and I know He has. He has also given me the assurance that the wallet *will be found,* and I'm willing to trust Him. I refuse to worry any more about it. So let's wipe those worry wrinkles off our faces, because the Lord knows exactly where that wallet is, and He'll bring it out of hiding in His own time. I just praise the Lord for His forgiveness, and for a family who is willing to forgive me. And I also thank you very much.

"With God's help," Clint continued, "I want to get victory over those bursts of temper like you saw last night. Please pray for me. Now come, let's eat supper. I couldn't eat all day, but now I'm hungry, and I hope you are too."

Their family worship that evening was a special time of earnestly imploring the Lord to reveal the missing wallet.

The next evening, the church group met in Ellen's home for Bible study and prayer time. The leader asked, "Does anyone have a special prayer request?"

A number of requests were given, and then little Shi-Enne's voice spoke up. "Please, pray that the wallet will be found." Later during prayer time, she joined in with a short prayer. "Please, Lord, help the wallet to be found."

God looked down and heard. Many hearts were touched by the faith of one little child. Likely one of Satan's helpers was hiding back in the shadows with doubled fist and clenched teeth, seething with hatred. Oh, how he longed to destroy these Christians, but the All-powerful One was holding him back.

\* \* \* \* \* \* \* \* \*

After the children were in bed, the phone rang. It was Darlene's mother. After visiting briefly, her mother said quietly, "The wallet is found."

Darlene was stunned. "Mum," she croaked, "what did you say?"

"The wallet is found," her mother repeated.

"When, where, how? Tell me all about it," sputtered Darlene, almost too excited to talk.

"Darlene, I feel terrible about putting your family through this trouble. I must be getting forgetful. I remember now that I had removed my wallet to get out some cash. And then I failed to replace it."

"Mum, don't worry about that, just tell me where it was," Darlene urged, pressing her ear tightly against the receiver.

"Well, I was using a toothpick when it flipped out of my hand and slid down between the cushion and the arm of my recliner. I slid my hand down to retrieve it, but instead of the toothpick, I came up with my wallet. All my money and cards were still there, Darlene. I was so glad to find it, but I feel terrible about the grief I caused to your family."

"Oh, Mum, all is forgiven. Praise the Lord! Oh, I'm so happy, praise the Lord!" shouted Darlene.

"Yes, praise the Lord!" agreed her mother.

"Mum, I've got to go and tell Clint. Oh, he'll be happy!"

Darlene ran into her bedroom and threw her arms around Clint's neck. "I've got wonderful news!" she squealed. "The wallet is found! I'm sorry I ever doubted you."

Clint looked at her in a daze. "What are you saying? Tell me again."

"Oh, Clint, I'll tell you later, but I've got to call the pastor's wife. This is great news!"

The joyful news was shared with the pastor and then his wife, and the words, "Praise the Lord!" were fervently repeated many times.

"Norma," Darlene said, "when Clint knew the wallet was found, he didn't say, 'I told you you'd regret doubting me.' He has such a forgiving attitude toward my mother and sisters. He just said, 'We need to keep praying for them.'

"That is thrilling, Darlene," agreed Norma, "and you will keep on growing into the image of our Lord. Darlene, do you remember Clint's dismissal prayer last Sunday night?

"Yes."

"I was struck by one thing he prayed. He said, 'Lord, keep each of us from the evil one, the roaring lion, who goes about seeking to devour us.' "

"Well," replied Darlene, "the roaring lion tried his best to devour our family this week, but our God is all-powerful. Praise the Lord!"

# 70

## God Showed the Way

*Norma Plank*

Once while we lived in Puerto Rico, my husband Don and I were driving down a street not far from our house in Parcelas Tiburón. We passed a woman walking on the sidewalk. She had beautiful long black hair done up in a bun. Her dress was very modest.

"Oh, look at that woman!" I told Don. "I wish we could meet her. She looks so nice."

"But we don't know where she lives, and we can't stop now," Don said.

"Yes, I know, and a woman walking on a sidewalk could live anywhere," I agreed, disappointed.

Day after day, the Lord kept bringing this woman to my mind. I knew the Lord wanted me to try to find her. But how could I?

A few weeks later, Alicia, a dear black lady who was bilingual, came from Añasco to spend several days with us and go visiting with me in the homes in Tiburón. I was far from fluent in Spanish, but together we made a team, and it was a joy to work with Alicia.

We had just finished visiting in a home and were considering where to go next, when the Lord placed a heavy burden on my heart to find the lady I had seen on the sidewalk.

I turned to Alicia. "A few weeks ago I saw a lady walking along the sidewalk. The Lord won't let me forget her. I know where I saw her, but I have no idea where she lives. Let's walk to that street and pray as we go that the Lord would lead us to her."

Alicia also believed that God answers prayer, so we prayed as we walked. Soon we were on the right street. I kept a sharp lookout for the dark-haired lady.

Suddenly my heart leaped, for I saw her on top of a flat-roofed house! I grabbed Alicia's hand and said quietly, "There she is, hanging up her clothes, and she's looking at me." In my excitement, I threw up my hand and waved.

When we got closer, she came to the edge of the roof, and I made the mistake of saying, "Hello, there," instead of saying, *"Buenas dias, Señora."*

To my amazement and delight, that woman replied in English. I felt like weeping for joy, because Don and I had been praying that God would lead us to bilingual people on the island.

We introduced ourselves, and then I said, "I can see you are very busy today. But may we visit sometime soon?"

She said, "Sure, come back this evening. My husband and I will be glad to visit with you."

My heart overflowed with praise to God as we walked home. *What a mighty God we have! He heard our prayer and prepared the way before us so that we not only found this special woman but also received an invitation to visit her. "Marvelous are thy works; and that my soul knoweth right well."* It was exciting to share the news with Don when we returned home.

That evening, Don, Alicia, and I had a wonderful visit in that home. We learned that their names were Rafael and Altagracia Gonzales, and they both loved the Lord. Altagracia's husband and friends called her Teté. We became close friends and shared meals in each other's homes. If we didn't visit them at least once a week, they'd call us and say, "Come over! We have something for you and want you to come and pick it up."

They started attending our worship services and would often go along when we had cottage meetings in various homes. They were a great blessing to us from God.

Several years later, Rafael went to meet his Maker. Teté still faithfully attends our church in Puerto Rico and continues to be a blessing, though her health is failing.

"Thank You, God, for leading us to these people."

# 71

## Yes, God Still Speaks Today

*Norma Plank*

Sunday dinner was over and the dishes cleared away, and I had just lain down for a nice nap. But for some reason I couldn't settle down, which was very unusual.

Finally I said, "Lord, what is the matter? Is there something You want to tell me?"

The Lord prompted me strongly, "Get ready for children's meeting at the evening church service."

"But, Lord," I argued, "I don't even know if they're having a children's meeting this evening. If they are, they would already have appointed someone."

The Lord gave me no rest. He said, "Yes, someone was supposed to be notified, but they forgot to tell the person."

I am sorry to say I couldn't believe the Lord was actually telling me these things, and I didn't prepare. *It's surely just my imagination,* I thought.

That evening I entered the church with fear and trembling. I desperately wished I had come prepared, because those promptings were still very real.

The service began with two songs followed by a short devotional. Then Tilman Bear, the moderator, called for the children to come forward and announced that Louise Bear would have children's meeting. All was quiet, and no one responded. Finally Louise's father spoke up and said, "I'm sorry. I was supposed to notify her, but I forgot."

By then, I was really shaken up; that's what the Lord had told me in the afternoon. I dropped my head and thought, *If I don't look at Tilman, surely he won't call on me to be an impromptu substitute.*

But he said, "Norma, will you have something for the children?"

Ordinarily I can think of a Bible story for children, but this time I shook my head. I knew I was too upset and would only get up there and weep.

If I remember right, Tilman didn't want to disappoint the children, so he led them in some songs. Then he called for the first topic of the evening, which was entitled "Does God Speak Today?"

When I heard the title of the topic, I was overwhelmed. Now I understood why the Lord had spoken to me that afternoon. I was trembling before this all-knowing God; *why hadn't I listened to Him?* I begged the Lord to forgive me and promised to confess my sin at the first opportunity.

At the end of the service, Brother Tilman asked, "Is there anyone here who has something to say?"

I thought, *Oh, no, Lord! I'm not emotionally able. I just can't tonight.* I'm sorry to say that I failed to keep my promise. I didn't confess my sin, the meeting closed, and I felt very discouraged.

A week later, the minister in charge announced the program for the following Sunday night. When he named who would have children's meeting, the Lord prompted me again. He said, "You will be having that children's meeting; I'm giving you another chance."

This time I said, "Lord, You heard them say another person will have that responsibility. But You are all-knowing; and if I'm asked, I am willing to tell the children my experience of how God does speak today. And I'll tell them how sorry I am because I didn't listen to You the first time."

It came as no surprise when I received a call later in the week, asking me to prepare something for children's meeting. I'm happy to say that I was faithful in keeping my promise this time. But I would feel much better if I could say that I listened when God spoke the first time.

# VII.

GOD SPEAKS THROUGH MIRACULOUS

*Ways*

# 72

## *She Being Dead Yet Speaketh*

*Wilma Hofer*

One night I lay awake beside my sleeping husband, longing for sleep myself. We had just heard the shocking news that my dear husband had cancer (melanoma), and medically speaking he didn't have much time to live. He was a minister sixty-four years of age, and I was sixty. We had known of others afflicted with this dreaded disease, and we truly felt sorry for them. But now it was happening to us, and this was different. Yet even in this experience, we felt that God desired us to be a testimony for Him—which we truly wanted to be.

As I lay there troubled in spirit and unable to sleep, I suddenly heard the most beautiful music, along with these words: "Come to me, child of mine, and I will comfort you." I felt that it came straight from Heaven, and how comforting it was!

In the days that followed, I took this blessed assurance with me. I didn't tell anyone at first; it seemed like a holy secret between the Lord and me.

Years later, I found the same words and tune on Number 64 of *Life Songs #1,* under the title, "I Will Comfort You." After I read the song, I knew where these comforting words originated. My own dear mother sang them in the early days of my childhood. She often sang, and later I realized that she sang in spite of a burdened heart. Her lot in life was not easy, but she chose to sing instead of complain. She didn't know that God would use her song to bless her child nearly sixty years later.

With great awe and reverence I realized God had reached back into my childhood memories and brought me those comforting words in my hour of need.

Does God still speak? Yes, He certainly does, and with that assurance comes a feeling of great unworthiness. How is it that this great and holy God stoops to care for His creatures, who are but dust, and He desires to be our loving heavenly Father? "Amazing grace, how sweet the sound!" Here are the first stanza and chorus of the song.

I Will Comfort You

When the day is sad and drear,
And the life is full of care;
When no friend is nigh to cheer,
And the burdens hard to bear,

Chorus:
Listen! A voice divine,
Whispers its message true—
Come to me, child of mine,
And I will comfort you,
Come to me, child of mine,
And I will comfort you.

—Hattie H. Pierson

# Up? Down? How Does Gravity Work?

*Carolyn Roth*

It was Thursday afternoon, the day for Bible study. My husband was in the mountains for three days, teaching pastors. I stayed home in Managua with our five-year-old daughter and our son of eighteen months. A cheerful teenager came to accompany us to the Bible study and to help me care for the children.

The meeting place was on the other side of town, an hour-and-a-half away by bus. Crowded city buses mandated light traveling. We carried only an extra diaper in a plastic bag, the house key, and the bus fare. I also had two extra coins in my skirt pocket.

Yamileth carried the baby, and I took my daughter by the hand as we left the house under the sweltering midday sun.

After Bible study and prayer with the ladies, we visited while drinking tall glasses of ice-cold lemonade. Then the four of us hurried to catch the 4:00 p.m. bus before the workers at the milk plant across the highway ended their workday and packed all the buses like sardines in a can.

Once on the crowded bus, we made our way to the back for an easier exit at our transfer. Wanting to reassure myself, I felt in my pocket for the bus fare. Yes, it was there—but where was the house key? The key was not there! Further investigation revealed a tiny hole in the corner of the pocket, barely as large as the key.

My heart sank as I breathed a prayer for wisdom and quickly reviewed the options: *Check if the key has fallen onto the floor of the packed bus. (Impossible.) Retrace our steps to our friend's home and look there. (Maybe.) Continue our trip home, and beg the neighbors to help us break into the house through the back windows that are not covered with bars. (Not a pleasant prospect.)*

We decided to get off at the next stop and retrace our steps. Thank God for that extra fare! There beside the road we fervently prayed for a *miracle.*

Carefully we retraced our path from the bus stop to our friend's home. Nothing! No one there had seen the key or could offer any help. There was nothing to do but return to our house.

So we tearfully trudged back toward the highway. I said, "Yamileth, let's look again—every inch of the way!"

With our eyes fastened to the ground, we diligently scanned the dust and bits of grass that surely could not hide a key attached to a blue-gray string.

Suddenly I heard a clear command. "Look up!"

I pushed the thought aside and thought, *Keys fall down, not up.*

Again the command came. "Look up!"

*But if I take my eyes off the ground, I might overlook the very spot where the key is.*

The voice was insistent. "Look up!"

I looked up. There in front of me a man was hanging my key on the branch of a mimosa tree.

*"Mi llave!* (My key!)" I shouted.

"Oh, is this yours?" he responded kindly, handing me the *miracle.*

I was dumbfounded; then my words gushed forth. *"Sí! Sí! Gracias! Muchas gracias!* (Yes! Yes! Thanks! Many thanks!)" I stared at my precious key to make sure it was real, then turned to thank the man once again. But he was nowhere to be seen.

# 74

## After Eight Long Years

*Norma Plank*
*Rewritten by permission*

For eight years, a missionary woman had faithfully crossed the river dividing China from North Korea and traveled to a small town deep in North Korea to share the Gospel. It was hard, dangerous, and sometimes discouraging work, because the people were afraid to accept the Good News. They knew what happened to Christians— immediate imprisonment without a trial. The sentence could be for many years, and many Christians never came out alive.

In spite of their fears, people were attracted to the missionary. This was not because of the gospel message, but because she often brought clothes, food, or other goods not easily found in North Korea. The people lived in great need, for the political and economic situation in

North Korea was so fragile. With no hope and little to lose, they gave themselves to stealing and violence to keep body and soul together.

Once again the missionary crossed the river and entered North Korea. Something told her that this visit would be different. *I feel God is going to do something special tonight,* she thought. *Somehow the Good News will reach these hopeless people, but it will be with a great risk on my part.* Her pulse quickened.

She prayerfully entered a small room filled with people who had gathered to receive her gifts. The Holy Spirit moved her to approach an old lady whose hand was shriveled into a useless claw. Suddenly faith leaped within the missionary. "Will you believe in Jesus if He heals you today?" she asked boldly.

The crippled old lady hesitated thoughtfully; she had nothing to lose. She nodded her head, but her face showed no expectation. People moved closer as the missionary began to pray.

Time crept by slowly, and sweat trickled down the missionary's back. Nothing was happening. She began crying out in a loud voice, pleading for God to show His power and His mercy.

Suddenly someone in the crowd shrieked, "It's moving! Her hand is opening!"

Every eye in the room was focused on the crippled hand.

The old woman was crying, "My hand—my fingers—they are straightening out! Oh, she must be right!"

"What she teaches must be true," the group murmured.

As the missionary wiped the sweat off her face with a towel, another lady came up and asked, "Can you come to our house and ask your God to heal my husband?"

The missionary was exhausted from the spiritual struggle, but she found herself saying, "Yes, let's go." *God is going to do something more to capture the hearts of these people, His lost sheep,* she thought.

The whole group walked across town in the darkness. They found the woman's husband, a medical doctor, lying on the floor. He had fallen three years ago, and since then he could not walk, stand, or move freely.

When the doctor heard about his wife's plan, his eyes flashed with anger. He shouted, "I have studied modern science! Only science heals, and I cannot be healed. God is a myth. I will not allow this woman to touch me."

The missionary prayed, "Shall I lay my hands on this man for healing?"

She heard the reply. "I will be with you."

She started telling him about Jesus, and how He had healed many sick and crippled people. "If you believe, Jesus will heal you."

A change took place in the man; a glimmer of hope came to his eyes. Finally he nodded his head.

The missionary gently placed her hand on his shoulder and began to pray. "Dear God, heal this doctor so that he may know that You are greater than medicine." She went on praying fervently.

Everyone was silent, wondering what would happen.

*Would he be healed like the woman at the other house?*

Suddenly the doctor's body began moving. "This is not real!" he cried out. "It is not me!" He sat up and struggled to stand.

The watching people were amazed. "Who is this God, that He has such power?" they said softly.

Standing on his feet, the doctor said tearfully, "Now I believe. Yes, yes, Jesus is better than any medical surgeon."

People were clapping and crying—but softly, for fear someone might hear and report them.

After eight long years of work with no visible results, the missionary was blessed to see *all* the people who witnessed God's power bow down before Him. They proclaimed their acceptance of God as their Lord and Master.

The doctor's final promise made the missionary's eyes shine before she left. He said, "We will meet in our house regularly and worship God every Sunday."

The night was late and the missionary had to leave the country before any rumors brought the police to investigate. As she wearily walked the dangerous journey toward home, she was overwhelmed by the love of her God. She felt God's comfort, like a warm stream flowing through her chilled body as she heard the words, "Well done, my good and faithful servant."

\* \* \* \* \* \* \* \*

In recent years God has been displaying His power in North Korea through signs and wonders like these, building His church as He chooses. Many small groups of believers worship the risen Lord in secret. They gather in the wilderness, on mountain slopes, behind barns, and in other hidden places to avoid being seen by the police. Because of God's work through faithful missionaries in border towns, the underground church is multiplying.

# Return of the Prodigal Daughter

*Norma Plank*
*Names have been changed for privacy*

Preacher Smith and his wife were deeply troubled. Their precious daughter Judy had become infatuated with a non-Christian man, and she was about to go out the door with a suitcase in each hand.

"Please, Judy, turn away from this man," pleaded her father. "He doesn't love the Lord, and you are heading for much unhappiness if you go with him."

Judy steeled herself against her mother, who was sobbing in a chair close by. She turned to answer her father.

"But I love him, Daddy, and I've promised to go with him to New York. Don't try to stop me, because I'm going," Judy declared.

"Judy, dear," said her father with tears streaming down his cheeks, "We are trying to spare you from sorrow, but you have refused our help. Some day you will find your-self at the bottom. Then please remember to cry out to God, and He will help you."

Judy left without looking back. But after six years with this wicked man, she was very sorry for what she had done. Yet in all that time, she refused to humble herself and call her parents. They did not know she now had three children: Mark (6), Esther (4), and five-month-old Lillian. Judy and the children were little more than skin and bones from lack of food. The baby was sick and cried continuously. Little Esther had a terrible fear of men because of being cruelly mistreated and molested by her father, who was now in prison.

Judy was sick of her life. One day she decided, "This is enough. I'm going home to my mom and dad." She put her children's belongings into some plastic bags, and gathered what money she could find. Then they piled into her old car and left New York for Tennessee.

On an interstate highway in Pennsylvania, a tire blew out. A state police officer called a service truck to replace it, but it cost more than she had on hand. She heaved a grateful sigh when the service man agreed to pay the last few dollars. Judy drove on. Then a new problem developed. Nearing a rest area in Tennessee, she noticed smoke rolling out from under the hood.

"Oh, what shall I do—this car must be on fire!" Judy gasped. She sped into the rest stop, sprang out, and quickly pulled the children out. Then she herded them to a picnic table a safe distance from the car.

Judy bowed her head over her crying baby and thought, *I'm at the end. I don't know what to do next.* It was then that she suddenly remembered her father's words. "When you're at the bottom, cry out to God. He will help you."

Judy's shoulders shook with sobs as she cried out to God for help—the very One she had forsaken six years ago. Suddenly God revealed to her that He would make a way for her by sending a man driving a brown semitruck. *But, Lord, how will I know which truck if there should be several brown ones?* The Lord made it clear to Judy that the brown truck would park near the steps at slot number 27, and the driver would help her. So Judy and her children sat and waited for God to show Himself strong.

* * * * * * * * *

Mr. and Mrs. Sandy Driver had just read a Scripture and prayed together for God's guidance and safety. Sandy hauled mail with a tractor trailer and would be gone for two days. He gathered up his lunch and a bag containing his Bible and a devotional book, along with some New Testaments, gospel tapes, and CDs for distribution.

"I'll keep in touch with my cell," he called. With a cheery wave to Martha, he drove to the postal facility where his truck was parked.

When he arrived, Sandy took the steering wheel of a large brown Mack truck. He would be pulling a white fifty-three foot trailer with a load of mail on his regular run to Clinton, Tennessee. Sandy bowed his head and prayed, "Please protect me, Lord, and help me to take advantage of any opportunity You might send my way. I know that without You I can do nothing, but I will count it a privilege to be an instrument in Your hand. I ask this through Jesus' name. Amen."

Sandy wasn't expecting anything unusual, but wanted to take advantage of any opportunity to be a testimony for God. Sandy often stopped at the rest stop at mile marker 75 on Interstate 81, just across the state line in Tennessee. But today Sandy felt impressed to go on to the next rest stop, at the 41-mile marker. He didn't like stopping there as well because he had to climb a long uphill grade when he left to continue south on Interstate 81. But he had learned to mind the inner promptings of the Spirit.

Sandy pulled slowly into the rest stop. Today it was almost full of parked trucks. Noticing an open slot near the steps, he pulled into it. As was his custom, he locked the brakes, got out, and walked around his truck, checking tires, lights, and hoses.

He had just completed his inspection when he noticed some people sitting at a picnic table. A young boy came running from the picnic table toward him. The boy stopped as Sandy neared the steps. "Are you my grand-daddy?" the boy asked.

"No," Sandy replied. "I'm not *your* granddaddy, but I am a granddaddy."

The boy clutched two of Sandy's fingers, and they climbed the steps together. As they reached the top, a woman with a small girl and a crying baby came to meet them.

"We've been waiting for you for three hours," said the woman. "When the smoke started rolling out of my car, I knew I was at the end of my rope. Then I remembered what my preacher daddy said, 'When you get to the bottom, cry out to God and He will help you.' So I prayed and the Lord told me a man in a brown truck was going to park in slot number 27, near the steps, and he would help me."

Sandy swung around and looked toward his truck. Sure enough, he was parked in slot number 27, quite near the steps. He hadn't stopped here to work on someone's car, but he did know how to fix some things.

"Well, let's have a look at your car," he said. The little boy was still hanging on to Sandy's two fingers.

Sandy raised the car hood and noticed right away that a heater hose had burst. That had caused a cloud of steam—not smoke as the woman had thought. After several trips to his truck for tools and antifreeze, Sandy shortened the hose and rerouted it. He then added antifreeze and water.

While Sandy worked on the car, Mark and Esther began crying. "We're hungry, Mommy," they said.

"Hush now, please don't cry," Sandy heard their mother say. "I don't have money to buy anything. We will eat at granddaddy's house after a while."

Sandy soon learned that the little boy's name was Mark, the fearful little girl was Esther, and the baby was

Lillian. The mother's name was Judy Jones. Since Sandy dearly loved children, he was deeply touched by the cries of these little ones. He turned to Judy and asked, "Are your children hungry?"

She nodded her bowed head and began weeping. Piece by piece the sad story came out—how Judy had left home against her parents' wishes nearly six years before; how they had not heard from her since.

"Do your mom and dad know you're on your way home?" Sandy asked.

Judy shook her head.

Sandy looked at this pitiful family. The children were filthy. Except for pictures from foreign countries, he had never seen skinnier children. The mother had a terribly swollen and bruised cheek, and several teeth were missing. He had seen several black plastic trash bags in the car and assumed they contained all Judy's earthly belongings. And she had no money.

Judy excused herself to go to the restroom with her crying baby to tend to its diaper and fill her bottle with water.

Mark stayed close to Sandy. "Did you eat breakfast this morning, Mark?"

"No," Mark answered, "but we're gonna eat at granddaddy's after a while."

It would be close to six hours before they would arrive at their granddaddy's house near Chattanooga. He had also noticed that Judy had no clean diaper with her. When she returned with her girls, Sandy asked about it.

"No," Judy explained, "I had to rinse her diaper out and dry it under the blow-dryer where people dry their hands." The baby continued crying as she spoke.

Sandy's heart was wrung with pity, but he was in a dilemma. His load of mail had to be delivered on schedule, and he had already spent thirty or more minutes with Judy. But he couldn't just walk away, so he said, "Judy, load your children in your car and drive to the large truck stop at mile marker 36. I will buy your family something to eat before you travel on. I believe your car will run," Sandy explained before returning to his truck. "But you won't be able to use the heater."

Judy had never been at a service area as large as the Davy Crockett Truck Stop. Sandy waved her over to the gas pumps and filled up her gas tank; then he pointed out a place for her to park. She thought Sandy had circled around the truck stop and left without keeping his promise. By the time he found them, she and her children were all crying. When they were finally inside, Sandy noticed that the daily special was vegetable soup and cornbread—"All you can eat."

"I know from experience that the vegetable soup here is really good," he said.

"That sounds wonderful to me," Judy replied. "You are very kind, and I'm so thankful."

While the family was eating, Sandy told the cashier that he had fifty-four dollars and would like to buy some things this family needed. She helped pick out things Judy and her children would need, and even gave him a discount.

"Thank you for your help," Sandy said to the cashier. "Please keep the packages here at the checkout, and I'll tell the lady to pick them up."

Then Sandy walked over and laid a pencil and paper beside Judy. "Do you remember your daddy's phone number? I'd like to call him and let him know you're on your way."

After writing down the number, Judy said, "This was their number six years ago. I hope they still live there and their number hasn't changed. My daddy's name is Roy Smith, and he's a preacher."

Sandy called the number.

A man answered, "Hello. Roy Smith speaking."

Sandy cleared his throat. "I'm calling to let you know that your daughter Judy is on her way home."

"Really? That's wonderful news! We've been deeply burdened for her all day, and we took time to pray several times. We haven't heard from her for such a long time."

"Well," informed Sandy, "she's on her way with her three children."

Sandy heard Roy gasp and call excitedly to his wife. "Alyssa, come here! Judy's coming home, and she has three children." Sandy heard someone pick up another phone.

"Is Judy all right?" asked Roy, concern in his voice.

"No," Sandy said, "she's not all right. They are out of money, dirty, and malnourished. I think Judy has an abscessed tooth, or else she has been beaten and abused. Her cheek is swollen and several teeth are missing. They will need a lot of help. I filled her car with gas and bought supper for her and the children. I've also supplied her with Pampers, formula, and some other items. But I really can't do much more, because my work is time-sensitive, and I must be on my way."

"I'm so grateful for what you have done. Please give me your name and address so I can pay you back for helping our daughter," begged Roy.

"No, I really believe God wanted me to do this for her. It had to be an act of Providence that I even stopped at that rest area, because I usually avoid that one," said Sandy. "I'm just glad I could help your daughter."

"I certainly thank you, mister. Mom and I will come to meet Judy. We're so anxious to see her and the children. Where would be a good place to meet her?" asked Roy.

Sandy thought a moment. "A good place would be close to mile marker 398 on Interstate 40 at the Strawberry Plains exit near Knoxville, about two hours away."

"That sounds good. Tell Judy we'll be there. Thanks again for all your trouble, mister," said Roy.

After hanging up, Sandy smiled at the happiness in Roy's voice. The prodigal was coming home! And the parents were running to meet her! Judy's eyes lit up when she learned that her mother and father were on their way.

* * * * * * * * *

When Sandy shared his experiences with Martha, they rejoiced together over their merciful and all-powerful God.

Some time later Sandy contacted the Roy Smith family to see how the family was doing. Roy reported that Judy had made peace with God and the church, and the church was helping Judy get a home. Also, one of the members had a job for her.

As for the children, Mark was enrolled in school and doing well. Baby Lillian had to be hospitalized because of malnutrition. Little Esther needed corrective surgery due to repeated abuse at the hands of her father and possibly others. The father would be in prison for a long time.

*Will this man ever be converted and reunited with his family?* Sandy wondered. *God alone knows. I'm so relieved that Judy and her children have someone to care for them spiritually and physically. What a mighty God we serve!*

## Were They Angels?

*Dan Miller*
*As told to Norma Plank*

"Well, son, we need to make one or two more deposits in the bank, and then we'll be all set to buy our own farm." Father and son were going to town in their horse and buggy. It was in the 1920s, and things had been going well for the Miller family.

"That's great, Dad!" Ten-year-old Danny looked up at his father with shining eyes. "Maybe then I can have my own pony and cart."

"Not right away, Danny, but maybe sometime you can have a pony of your own." Dad guided the horse to the hitching rack in front of the bank. "Want to come along with me and see how the bank keeps our money safe?"

Danny stared wide-eyed as Dad showed him the huge safe, which the tellers locked tightly every night. This assured him that their money was safe, and they would soon own their dream farm.

On their trip home, Dad asked, "Would you like to hold the lines awhile, Danny? It's time for you to learn how to drive a team, because I'll be counting on you to be my right-hand man when we buy that farm." Danny flashed his dad a happy smile as he eagerly grasped the lines.

Two months later Dad and Danny made another trip to town. It was a happy trip until they came in sight of the bank. What was going on? A mob of angry people was milling around on the boardwalk in front of the bank. Everyone seemed to be talking at once, and several men were trying to force the door open.

"Dad, what's going on?" gasped Danny, grabbing the dashboard and leaning forward. "Hey, there's a big sign in the window."

Dad peered closely at the sign and read, "Permanently closed!"

"What does that mean?" gulped Danny. "They've got our money in there, Dad. Why are they closed?" Danny's fearful eyes waited for an answer.

"I really don't know, Danny. There's no place to tie our horse, so you stay here and hold the lines, and I'll see if I can find out. All right?"

"Sure, Dad, I'll stay, but look at those men over there. They look awfully angry. They won't hurt you, will they?" Danny asked, his forehead wrinkled with concern.

"Don't worry, Danny. Just pray," comforted Dad.

Danny watched his dad walk over to some men. The men were all talking at the same time. They stamped their feet and pounded their fists into the palms of their hands. Some men were crying, while others shook their fists at the sky. Never had Danny seen grown men behave like this. It was frightening. His dad returned slowly to the buggy, head bowed. Was he praying?

Dad sighed wearily as he climbed into the buggy. "Well, son, if those men are right . . . " He paused and swallowed hard. "We've lost the money we were saving for a farm." He leaned over and squeezed Danny's knee. "But let's keep our faith in God, Danny. He will see us through, because He's made many wonderful promises. And remember, it's impossible for God to lie."

Tears slipped down Danny's face, and he pressed his hand hard over his quivering lips. Now there would be no farm— no pony—nor would he be working daily beside his dad.

"Danny," comforted Dad, "there's nothing wrong with shedding a few tears." Dad pulled out his big hanky and handed it to Danny while brushing a tear from his own cheek. "It would be wrong, though, to let our hearts turn bitter against God. He will take care of us. And, Danny, we have each other. I'd rather lose this money than to lose you or some other member of our family. We still have much to be thankful for, don't we?"

"But, Dad, I can't understand why God would let this happen. We've been saving and working so hard. Sure, I'm glad we didn't lose anyone in our family, but I wanted a farm so much." Danny buried his face in Dad's hanky.

"At least we have the money we were going to deposit, so we're not penniless—and I still have a job," Dad said.

"Let's try to be as cheerful as we can, Danny. That will be a help to the rest of the family, and I need your help."

The next morning Dad left for work as usual, but an hour later he returned. Danny met him at the door. "What's wrong, Dad? Are you sick?"

"No, son, I've lost my job. You see, many other people lost money too, so they cannot pay me for my work," explained Dad. "I want all of you to pray for me while I try to find another job."

"We'll certainly be praying," assured Mom. "Shall I write to my parents? They might know of a job out their way. It's a much larger community."

"Yes, please do that," agreed Dad, and he hurried away.

The news wasn't good when Dad returned in the evening. Jobless men were everywhere looking for work. Each day was the same—no job and no way of making money.

A week later, Danny raced into the house, yelling, "Mom, here's a letter from Grandma!"

"Oh, I hope it's good news. Get my specs, Danny," urged Mom as she settled into her rocker and reached for a hairpin to slit the envelope.

Danny watched his mother as she peered through her glasses and carefully read the letter. "What does she say, Mom?" he asked.

"Well, she says she doesn't know of a job right off, but she believes there would be a better chance of finding work in their large community. Also, she says we can live rent-free in the little house on their property. We'll show the letter to your dad this evening." Mom tucked the letter into her apron pocket.

After supper Mom handed the letter to Dad. "Hmm-m, a rent-free house would be a big help right now," he said. "I believe this is an answer to our prayers. Danny, tomorrow you can help Mom with the packing, and I'll see if I can borrow a team and wagon to move our furniture. We'll dig our potatoes, and let's not forget the cords of wood. Both will come in handy, I'm sure. Another thing, let's not forget to thank God for supplying our need at this time. Now let's help Mom get this kitchen cleaned up, and then off to bed we go. Tomorrow will be a big day."

Moving day came and went. It was a tight squeeze to get everyone and everything moved into the tiny house, but no one complained. They were thankful for a roof over their heads. Day after day, Dad looked for a job. He met with one disappointment after another—no jobs anywhere.

The day finally came when the money and food were all gone. Danny was scared and hungry. He wondered, *Why doesn't God answer my dad's prayer for a job?*

There was no food for breakfast, but Dad left as usual to look for a job.

"Come, children," called Mom, "let's kneel right down here together and tell our kind heavenly Father about our needs. I know you children are hungry, and our God is not poor. He will show us what to do."

Mom held out her arms and embraced her four children, two on each side. Then she prayed earnestly, "Our precious heavenly Father, our money and our food are all gone, and I beg You to have mercy on Your hungry children. You've given us many wonderful promises, and it's impossible for You to go back on Your Word. We trust You fully and we thank You, for we know the answer will come. Help our faith to stay strong. In the precious name of Jesus we pray. Amen."

Suddenly there was a loud knock, and Mom hurried to open the door as the children crowded close behind. There stood two women. "This food is for your family," they said. They turned and left quietly while Mom stared at the food. She was so overcome with emotion that she couldn't speak.

The children helped her carry the food inside. There was a large bag of flour, as well as a bag of potatoes and two sacks of other grocery items. The children squealed with delight, while tears ran down Mom's cheeks.

"Ah, children, let's kneel again and thank our kind heavenly Father." Again Mom gathered her children in her arms while they poured out their heartfelt thanks to God.

When they stood to their feet, Mom exclaimed, "Oh, no! We're forgetting our manners. Where are those women? We must thank them. Danny, you're quick—run out to the road and see if you can see them. We want to tell them how thankful we are."

Danny flew out the door but was soon back, wearing a puzzled expression. "Mom, they're nowhere in sight. They couldn't have gone far, because they didn't come by horse and buggy. Didn't you know who they were, Mom?" asked Danny.

"No, Danny, I've never seen them before," said Mom reverently. "I'll fix some food for you hungry children, and then we'll run across the field and describe the women to Grandma. She'll probably know so we can properly thank them."

After Grandma heard their story and the description of the women, she said, "I know of no women living in this area who would fit that description. If they had no horse and buggy, they couldn't have come from too far away. Very strange indeed!"

"Maybe not so strange after all, and maybe they did come from afar. Remember," reminded Mom, "those women knocked on our door just as we finished praying. Unless we find out differently, I'll always believe they were angels sent from God."

As the family walked back home, Danny asked, "Mom, do you really think those women were angels?"

"Whoever they were, Danny, they were sent by God. Without a doubt, they could have been angels." Mom's voice shook with emotion.

"We serve a mighty God, don't we, Mom?" asked Danny with awe.

"Yes, He is truly all-knowing and all-powerful," agreed Mom.

# God's Ministering Spirits

*Stan O'Bannon*

My dad was a merchant seaman and was away so much that I hardly knew him at all. I was the oldest child, followed by a sister and two brothers. Mom was fifteen when she married my dad. Though he sent money, Mom just couldn't accept his being gone for months at a time.

When Dad did come home from a voyage, he and mom would quarrel, and then Dad would get angry and stomp out. I was four or five at this time. After these quarrels, my dad would sneak back into our house at night and take us children away—sometimes to his brothers and sometimes to his parents. They would hide us in dark closets and get guns and say they were going to kill my mom if she came and tried to get us back.

I could never understand why they put us in such *dark* closets. We were terrified, and it would seem like forever until we saw our mom again. Sometimes she successfully kidnapped us back. We were repeatedly snatched back and forth, which was terribly traumatic for us at such a young age.

While I was in first grade, I thought things were going pretty well between my mom and dad. But when I was in second grade, things came to a head. One morning I was getting ready to go to school when my mom called us all to the breakfast table. That was strange, because we never ate together—but there I was with Dad and Mom and my younger siblings. We were served oatmeal that morning; and to this very day, whenever I eat oatmeal, I think about that horrible morning.

When we were seated around the table, my mom said, "Your dad and I are getting a divorce, and you children need to decide which one you want to live with."

I was crushed. I didn't know how to spell *divorce,* but I knew what the word meant!

Right away my brother and sister said, "We'll go with Dad."

I remember saying, "I love you both, and I want to stay with both of you."

My mother said, "You can't do that. We're not going to stay together, so you need to decide."

"Mom," I said, "I don't want you to be by yourself, so I'll go with you."

Mom left the room crying. I had to go to school that morning, but I found it impossible to do my lessons—my mind whirled with uncertainties.

Shortly after my mom and dad's divorce, my mom married my stepfather. Then life really became a nightmare of bickering and fighting. I wanted to see my real dad, but my stepfather wouldn't let him be part of my life.

I didn't know it then, but I learned later that my dad would often drive past our house in the hope of seeing me in the yard. He knew he didn't dare stop. Everything seemed unfair, and I became very angry at life. I lived in constant fear that my mom or stepfather would get hurt in their fights. When I went to bed, I would pull the sheet over my head and cry and pray. I don't know where I got the concept of praying.

My family never went to church or prayed, yet my mom instilled in me some virtues that were right. She taught me to always be honest. She would sometimes mention God and the Bible. I couldn't figure out why, because we never went to church.

In my teens another fellow and I became good buddies at school. He and I went to church numerous times—first to one church and then another—looking for answers to life's problems. Then my buddy was in a car accident. I prayed to God that my buddy would live. But he died, and I was devastated.

The Vietnam War was on, and I had vivid dreams of being in the war and shot at. Also, hatred was building up in my heart toward my stepfather. I despised how harshly he treated my mom and us children. I knew I was special to Mom, who had been only sixteen when I was born. It seemed as if we had grown up together. Mom had more children by my stepfather; I was the oldest of her ten children.

Life wasn't good at all. I bought a pistol and promised myself that I would kill my stepfather when I turned eighteen. Things were getting really nasty between us. I started standing up to him and confronting him for being unfaithful to my mom. When my mom found out about his infidelity, I hated him even more.

I decided to leave home and stay with Willy's family. Willy was seven years my senior and a very close friend—one I really admired. He tried to help me even though he was not a Christian. In 1971 my draft number was sixty-five, and Selective Service kept notifying me that I was being drafted. I was frustrated with life, but, being in my senior year, I was determined to graduate from high school. At times I thought I would quit because life was so difficult.

Searching for answers to life's problems, Willy and I went to one church and then another. I was convinced there was a better way, but what was it?

Since I wasn't at home, I would occasionally call my mom to tell her that I loved her and that I was all right. My stepfather would grab the phone and curse me, saying that I should get home.

I would say, "I'll never come back. I hate you."

After school, I would work with Willy at a service station, pumping gas and fixing tires. One evening after work I was miserable and under heavy conviction, but I didn't know what to do about it. It was dark outside and the stars were shining. I remember raising my fist toward the sky and saying out loud, "God, if You can't reveal Yourself in a personal way so I can understand, just leave me alone; don't bother me anymore." Little did I realize what I was asking.

Willy and I went into his house and watched TV, and then went to bed. I slept on the couch. The next morning I went to school, still under heavy conviction. I went to work after school as usual. When I came home, it was snowing. After showering, we watched TV.

Suddenly the house shook three times, rattling the windows. What made it shake? There was no storm; it was just snowing. Suddenly three angels were in the room—one in front of me, one against the wall to my left, and one standing just behind me at the couch. I was petrified! Willy saw them too. I could hardly talk, but I stuttered, "Willy, do you see what I see?"

"Yes! What do they want?" he quavered.

I was terrified with a fear beyond words. The beings were pure white—purer than glistening white. Never before or since have I seen a white so pure. They simply stood there without saying a word. They had no wings, and they looked like men, not women. They wore long, flowing garments that reached all the way down to their bare feet.

The face of the angel in front of me was not distinct, as though a fog were over his features. He extended his hand toward me with his palm up and beckoned with his fingers for me to come.

"I don't understand," I said aloud.

The angel against the wall held a gold sword, and a gold chain was wrapped around his waist. With his right hand, he slanted the handle of the sword out, with the point still between his feet and his left hand resting on top of the sword hilt.

I said again, "I don't understand."

He nodded his head. I closed my eyes and saw myself in the future. Quickly I opened my eyes, shook my head, and said, "No, I can't do that." I looked at the angel again and repeated, "I can't do it." Again he put his hand out and beckoned me to come.

"Not if I have to do that," I said.

Again I closed my eyes and saw myself in another time period of my life. I could see myself doing what the angel was asking me to do, but again I shook my head and said, "No, I can't do that."

But the angel nodded his head encouragingly as if to say, "Yes, you can do it."

By this time I was shaking with sobs and could hardly talk.

Again the angel put his hand out, gesturing as though to say, "Are you going to come?"

Again I said, "I can't do it." I put my head down and saw myself again in still another setting. This one almost got the best of me. It frightened me so badly that my whole body was trembling. Finally I said, "I will, if you all promise to help me. Will you help me?" All three angels nodded their heads.

Again the house shook three times, accompanied with booms. Then the three angels were gone.

I fell on my knees in front of the couch, and there I sobbed and cried and prayed that God would help me. I felt so needy. But after what I had seen, I felt sure that I would receive help from God.

Willy sat quietly in his chair while all this was going on. When he saw me on my knees weeping, he came over, laid his hand on me, and asked, "Will you be okay? I'm going to leave you alone for now."

Unable to talk, I nodded. Willy went into the other room and shut the door. I stayed on my knees for a long time, sobbing and praying. I was completely soaked with sweat.

This is what I saw in the three visions. In the first, I was telling people about the Gospel and about the coming judgment day. I didn't feel qualified, because at that time I knew nothing about the Bible. I didn't even know that Genesis is the first book in the Bible. I didn't read the Bible, so I had no idea what the Bible said. I knew there is a God and a hell, but I didn't know God or His Word.

When I closed my eyes the second time, I saw more people, and I was asking them, "Are you faithful? If you have not been faithful in this life, you will miss eternity in Heaven."

The third time I saw terrible things. People had left the faith. They were turning away from God's Word; and I was pleading with them not to do that, because Christ would come as He promised. The reason they were leaving was because enemies were hunting them down. If

Christians were caught and refused to denounce the name of Christ, their heads would be cut off.

Then in the far distance I saw a city with many big buildings. The people in the city were happy—they were eating, drinking, and living in style—but it was in sin, gross sin. A person could go into that city, but he had to denounce the Christian life. If he refused, he was killed as described before.

After that I saw myself and many others in a desolate land with hardly any food. We were destitute, without even the necessary things of life. We were out there because we were determined to separate ourselves from wicked people and to be faithful to God and His Word.

I became a Christian through this experience, and today the things are happening that I saw. People are not faithful to God and His Word, and they are leaving the faith. That grieves me.

When I asked God to reveal Himself in a more personal way, I received much more than I had ever expected. But I'm so thankful that He was willing to reach down to me in my ignorance. God knew I was searching for Him and longed to know Him. He is no respecter of persons; we don't need to come from a solid Christian home to receive help from Him. I know now that the Bible says, "And ye shall seek me, and find me, when ye shall search for me with all your heart" (Jeremiah 29:13).

This experience has helped me stay faithful and to tell the gospel story to my neighbors and friends. Even though I feel very unworthy, God allowed me to see things the average person has not seen. No, I never drank. I was never on drugs. I wasn't sleeping or dreaming. I was awake, and those angels were very real.

* * * * * * * *

My mother's sister was married to Lloyd Hershberger. I began staying with them over weekends and helping him with his milk route. He was a big help in my Christian life. I noticed they had family devotions—Uncle Lloyd would read the Scriptures, the family would sing, and then they would kneel at the couch and pray. I remember asking my mom, "Why don't we do that?" But the idea didn't go over very well.

Willy and I continued going to a community church, but I was not receiving what my heart longed for. I wanted to grow closer to God. My prayer was that God would lead me to a church where I could serve Him and fulfill the call He gave me that night.

Then Uncle Lloyd invited me to the Mennonite church at Virginia Beach, and I soon saw they had what I wanted. I borrowed Uncle Lloyd's car and went to talk to his brother Joe Hershberger, who was a minister. Brother Joe took me into his study. I was very shy and scared of him.

He asked, "What is it that you'd like to talk about?"

I asked, "Could I join the church?"

He said, "First of all, have you received Christ as your Saviour?"

I said, "Yes, sir, I have." I realized I still needed to learn many things. But I knew without a doubt that Christ was living in my heart, and I wanted to live for Him.

I was accepted into an instruction class taught by some godly brethren. These men really knew the Scriptures, and they knew how to get close to God. I felt very ignorant of God's will, which caused me to be scared and nervous around these devout men.

Time kept moving and the draft wouldn't wait, so I never completely finished the instruction class. They baptized me anyway. But I was extremely shy, and I tried to convince Brother Joe that I couldn't give a public testimony. Before the baptismal service, we were back in a little room with the ministers and Simon Coblentz, the bishop. I'll never forget how he explained the whole procedure of the service.

Then he said, "By the way, Brother Joe informed us that you don't want to give a public testimony, and we'll honor that if you really feel you can't. But," he continued, looking over his glasses at me, "we also want you to know this, if the Lord has really done for you what you say He has, you can't help wanting to talk about it!"

After he said that, I was ready to share what the Lord had done for me. But I did not tell them about the three angels. That seemed too sacred, and even now I share it with great humility.

After the baptismal service, Simon Coblentz said, "Brother Stan, I just want you to know that everything you did here this morning was well and fine and good.

But it will not carry you all the way through into eternity. This is not the final answer."

I asked, "Do I need to study some more?"

He answered, "Well, yes, but what I mean is that you need to be faithful to your vows and develop solid convictions based on the Word of God. From today on, you must maintain your relationship with Christ and live out your convictions."

That really struck me and has been a big motivation in my Christian life. It didn't take me long to figure out which men in the church could help me grow so I could someday know the Bible as they did. I saw godly character in their everyday lives and in the way they served the church. I made it my goal to follow their examples and set my sights on the path they walked.

I would like to honor those dear brethren who loved and instructed me. I call Joe Hershberger my spiritual father. Uncle Lloyd Hershberger invited me to church. There are many others too—Norman Swartzentruber, Lester Nisly, Eldon Miller, Paul Overholt, Earl Schlabach, and Eli Yoder from Kansas (we named our son Eli after him). I'm mentioning these names to remind us all that people are watching our lives, and we need to be examples anyone can safely follow.

After Brother Joe explained the Scriptures on nonresistance, I believed we should not kill. I told the Selective Service board that I couldn't join the armed forces. It wasn't easy, but they finally agreed to let me serve time in 1-W service.

Several years later, the Lord blessed me with a wonderful Christian wife. One day, we invited my old buddy Willy into our home, and he and I went for a walk. "Willy," I asked, "did you see what I saw that night?"

"Yeah," he said, "you want me to describe them?" He described the very angels I had seen, but he had not seen my three visions.

I'm sorry to say that Willy is not a Christian to this day. "That experience was meant for you, not me," he said. I long for him to know the Saviour too.

After I saw the angels and committed myself to God, my attitude and goal for my stepfather completely changed. I wanted to see him saved. I sold the gun with which I had planned to kill him. I tried my best to establish a good relationship with him. Sometimes it was an extremely difficult struggle.

"I'm a man now," I told him, "and I'm going a different direction than you are. It is my desire that one day I will see you attending church and experiencing the joy that I have."

After several years, my mom and stepfather did start going to church. As long as they did, their home changed for the better.

My real dad passed away in 1990, my mom in 1991, and my stepfather in 2006—all of which were difficult times for me. I'm glad our heavenly Father is the final Judge of all who pass from this life. After the last breath is drawn, no one can change his eternal destination.

Many times I have considered that night when God revealed Himself to me in a personal way. God showed me that He is real, Heaven is a real place, and He does have a purpose for each of our lives. But we must remain faithful until we experience death or until Christ returns, or we will miss Heaven. That word *faithfulness* goes beyond church membership or attendance. It means sincerely following Christ and trying to carry out the work He has assigned to us. If we *are* faithful, we will hear these blessed words: "Well done, good and faithful servant; . . . enter thou into the joy of thy lord" (Matthew 25:23).

# 78

## God Comforts a Broken Heart

*Anonymous*

Our teenage daughter had made a poor choice of friends, with the result that she began rebelling against her parents, her God, and her church. Looking back, we realize that we could have done some things differently, but we were doing the best we knew how at the time. Her father and I had always required obedience in our home, but the day came when she decided to leave. She wanted more freedom.

My heart was broken; my tears flowed day and night. Every time I attended church services and the singing of hymns began, tears would stream down my cheeks. I wondered if I should stay at home until I had better control of my emotions. But then I thought, *No, I am in the presence of those who truly love me; surely they will understand.* And they did. Church services have always been important to me, but I felt a special need of the church during this time.

One day shortly after my daughter left home, I walked into my son's room to clean. I was so stricken with grief I hardly had strength to work but forced myself to keep going. I felt totally helpless, in a seemingly deep, dark hole with nowhere to look but up. Oh, how I needed encouragement!

In my son's room was a card table and on it lay an open Bible, a concordance, and a tablet with notations on various verses he had read. While calling to God for help, I picked up the open Bible and carried it to the window for better light. To my amazement, I experienced something that has never happened before or since. One verse stood out from all the rest. It seemed to be in larger, darker print.

The verse was Jeremiah 32:17. "Ah Lord GOD! behold, thou hast made the heaven and the earth by thy great power and stretched out arm, and there is nothing too hard for thee."

I could visualize Jeremiah, with arms outstretched toward Heaven, praying this marvelous prayer of faith. What was my Lord trying to tell me? Was He saying my daughter's problem was not too hard for Him to handle?

Her father and I had tried everything we could think of—fasting, praying, talking, and begging. We knew that in our own strength, we were helpless. But now, hope was again stirring in my heart. I was reminded that God is all-powerful and that He can do anything He pleases.

I longed after Jeremiah's kind of faith. Was God offering for us to totally trust our daughter's life into His hands?

We shuddered to think of the reaping ahead of her. No godly parent enjoys watching his or her children suffer. But if it would yield the peaceable fruit of righteousness, we were ready to say, "Yes, Lord, Your will be done."

I think the Lord saw that my faith was in need of an extra boost, because that very night after I finally fell asleep—again on a tear-soaked pillow—I suddenly heard a large choir singing. Never before or since have I heard such beautiful singing. The harmony was perfect, exuberant, joyful, love-filled, and heaven-sent. Every singer was putting his all into it, and I could tell that each one was fully convinced of the truth he was singing. It is impossible for me to describe the beauty.

They sang only one phrase: "'Tis true, oh, yes, 'tis true; God's wonderful promise is true." I knew without a doubt that they were telling me to put my faith and confidence wholly in this all-powerful God, who is able to do anything. I was so overcome with the beauty and the message of that heaven-sent music that I was unable to sleep anymore that night. Instead, I spent my time in weeping for joy and praising God, who is able to keep every one of His promises.

This experience was very real and precious. The next morning I asked my husband and children, "Did you hear the beautiful singing in the night?"

"We heard no singing," they all said. When I called my closest neighbors, they hadn't either. Then I knew this wonderful blessing was meant especially for me. I felt so tenderly loved by my Lord. Even today, many years later, I still cherish this experience, though I feel utterly unworthy of such love and mercy from this High and Lofty One—the King of kings and Lord of lords.

I used to wonder, *Whatever will we do to occupy our time throughout all eternity?* I no longer wonder. If one phrase sung by heavenly singers can cause such rejoicing and praise from me, I know all of God's children will be joyfully occupied in their heavenly home, with never a boring moment. Our praise and rejoicing will be completely spontaneous, and God has promised to wipe away all tears, whether they be sad or glad tears. My faith was greatly increased through these experiences.

I wish I could say my daughter made a quick turnaround and was brought back into loving favor in our home and with God and the church. But no; after so many years, she is still trying to find happiness in her own way.

I have not lost hope of her return. I am still clinging to that special verse in Jeremiah, which God gave to me in such a marvelous way. I am convinced that where there is life, there is hope, and that there is nothing too hard for my Lord. He will continue to work with our daughter on a daily basis in response to our earnest prayers. God is faithful.

# 79

# Donny Good's Battle With Leukemia

*Donny Good*

*Fear thou not; for I am with thee: be not dismayed;*
*for I am thy God:*
*I will strengthen thee; yea, I will help thee;*
*Yea, I will uphold thee with the right hand of my righteousness.*
Isaiah 41:10

The verse above has been a great inspiration to us. We never know God's plans for our lives, yet we know He is always there to help us if we seek Him.

I cannot put into words how much it meant to have the support of family and friends during my battle with leukemia. Mail time at the hospital was the highlight of our day. So often on a day we were discouraged, a card or letter would come with a Scripture verse or an encouraging word that was just what we needed. By the end of my first hospital stay, around 120 cards were hanging on the wall of my room. The doctors and nurses were impressed with how many people cared about us.

The first sign that anything was wrong came in November 2005, when I started losing my appetite and feeling unusually tired. At first we thought I was working too hard and not getting enough sleep. A chiropractor thought maybe my adrenal glands were the problem. By December I had lost about twenty pounds and was throwing up in the evenings. Nothing seemed to help. By the first of the year, I could hardly move one foot in front of the other.

A blood test was taken, and on January 12, 2006, we were told the bad news. I was to go the James Cancer Institute in Columbus, Ohio, as soon as possible. We were devastated. We called for our church leaders and had an anointing service that evening.

At the hospital the next day further tests confirmed I had a severe type of acute myelogenous leukemia, a cancer of the white blood cells. For the first few days we struggled tremendously with questions. "Why? Why us? Why me?"

We were also faced with a host of other things we had never considered before. Do you have a living will? Do you have a power of attorney in case anything happens? Do you realize you may never have any more children? *What—never have more children*! Suddenly our one little boy became doubly precious. *But God, we're young—only twenty-six—just starting our life together!*

How could we possibly handle everything that was being thrown at us? We quickly realized this wasn't going to be over with soon. Worries flooded our minds. What would happen to our house? How would we pay our bills? Who would take care of our animals?

But God was in control. Miracles started happening. On Sunday night we got a phone call saying my wife's cousin, Danny Wolfenbarger, was coming to live at our place and take care of it till I got better, no matter how long it took. We were amazed.

A few days later another miracle happened. Three different people visited us; and by the time they left, we had received enough cash for our next mortgage payment. It seemed God was saying "See, I have not forsaken you. I am here and taking care of you. Trust Me."

The doctors said aggressive treatment was necessary for me to have any chance of survival. They recommended a strong chemotherapy—a combination of three drugs, which they gave me twice a day for seven days. The treatment was to wipe out my cancerous white blood cells to almost nothing, then let my bone marrow rebuild new ones. The only problem is that chemo kills not only the bad white cells but also other cells in the body.

After the seven days my white cell count continued dropping, as did my red blood cells and platelets. A normal person has a white cell count of about 4,000 to 10,000. My white cell count was at 0.02. As my red cell count dropped, I was given blood transfusions to keep me alive. During my first hospitalization, I received a total of fifteen units of blood.

Almost two weeks into my stay, I had an unforgettable experience. The port in my neck through which chemo was administered became infected, causing a fever that proved to be a living nightmare for the next five days. The fever started at 106.5°F, then began a yo-yo effect that bounced between 103.0°F and 105.8°F. The nurses packed me in ice, had me take a cold shower, and even tried a cooling blanket through which cold water was circulated. Nothing worked.

Then I developed "rigors." As my fever rose, my body and legs would shake uncontrollably—so hard that the bed shook. My legs began cramping terribly for as long as forty-five minutes at a time. This happened repeatedly every hour or so. Morphine and other medications did nothing to dull the pain. At night when my body raged with fever, I would wake my wife, and she would bathe me with a cold cloth, trying to cool me. I don't know what I would have done without my wife and little boy. Just seeing them gave me a drive to live.

I continued growing weaker until I couldn't even get out of bed. It took all my energy just to roll from one side to the other. I would be so out of breath that I couldn't even talk. My heart rate was also increasing daily. It was at about 140 beats per minute, and my chest kept getting tighter and tighter. I remember my parents coming and visiting me, and when they left, I wondered if I would ever see them again.

In one stretch of three days and nights, I could not sleep at all. At night my room seemed to turn into a different world. Whenever I closed my eyes, I felt as if I were falling into a deep black pit. Lights flashed and flew past me as I fell. It terrified me so that I refused to close my eyes. I would sing and pray and recite Bible verses, like Isaiah 41:10, to keep from going berserk.

As I prayed and sang, an image of the cross of Jesus appeared on the wall where our cards hung. I would keep my eyes fastened to this image all night and think of these words: "The cross is not greater than His grace; / The storm cannot hide His blessed face. / I am satisfied to know, / That with Jesus here below, / I can conquer every foe." It felt as though God was right there in the room with me. I was reassured that with His help I could get through the night.

Finally on the fifth day my heart rate raced to 170. As a last resort they gave me a steroid shot that broke the fever, and immediately I started feeling better. My heart rate went down, and my blood counts started rising. Two-and-a-half weeks later I was able to go home. During the four-and-a-half weeks in the hospital, I had lost another twenty pounds. I was so weak that I could not stand for more than ten minutes or hold my little boy.

Treatment for my kind of leukemia usually involves two rounds of chemotherapy, with the second eliminating cancer cells that survive the first round. When I was strong enough, I would return to the hospital for the second round. The doctors wanted to follow the chemotherapy treatments with a bone marrow transplant.

Tests showed that neither my brother nor my two sisters were a match. Again we were devastated. The doctors said that without a transplant, I had only a twenty percent chance to live. But the doctors found a hundred possible matches with the National Bone Marrow Registry, which gave us some hope.

I did some research on bone marrow transplants, and I did not like what I found. I learned that to prepare me for the transplant, I would be given a very large amount of chemotherapy and then go through intense radiation. The purpose would be to kill my bone marrow and all the blood cells in my body. Then they would give me some bone marrow from someone else, which if my body accepted it, would grow and start producing normal blood cells. There are numerous potential side effects, both short-term and long-term, from this type of a transplant. The more I researched, the more frightened I became. We began to call on God to please show us what to do.

On March 13 I returned for the second round of chemotherapy, and once again my counts began to drop. But this time treatments went much better. I didn't get as sick, and I had only a low-grade fever for about two days.

A very common side effect of chemotherapy is sores in the mouth. The drugs ravage the digestive system, and one can get sores all the way through the digestive tract. The doctors said no one ever gets away without at least having mouth sores. But I never had any. I believe it was another miracle, for which I am very thankful.

What to do about the transplant was still a tremendous burden on us. What if the doctors couldn't find a donor? What about the horrible side effects? Was this really what we should do? Was there any other way to fight this thing? The doctors were having a hard time finding a match, because I had a rare blood type. What more could go wrong?

It was disturbing each day to hear "Code Blue" and know that someone was dying. We saw three different people die right across the hall from my room. It was very hard for us to sleep on those nights. Was this how I would die? What would my wife do? How could my little boy grow up without a daddy? *God, please don't let me die!*

When these times seemed overwhelming, we would sing and pray together. Many times we spent most of a day singing and praying, trying to keep our spirits up. "God Hath Not Promised" became our theme song, and we would sing it every day. We clung to Proverbs 3:5, 8: "Trust in the LORD with all thine heart; . . . It shall be health to thy navel, and marrow to thy bones."

Some days I felt as if God had abandoned me, and I couldn't feel His presence at all. On those days I would read my Bible and sing all the more. I knew Satan was waging war against me, and I wasn't going to let him win. As I would press into God's Word, I would finally feel the presence of God again.

One night after discussing what to do about a transplant, we decided to give the whole thing totally into the Lord's hands. We spent a long time in prayer, asking God to show us if there was any other way to fight my cancer. We learned that when we come to a place of total submission to God, we need to be ready, because the Lord wastes no time.

A miracle occurred the very next day. A total stranger called to share his testimony. He didn't tell me what to do or how to do it, but simply shared what the Lord had done for him. He had been diagnosed with leukemia ten years earlier. He was a strong Christian and decided to put everything into the Lord's hands. He went to his church and they prayed that the Lord would heal him. He has never had leukemia since. It was very encouraging.

This man had heard about me three weeks before, but decided not to call until the Lord told him to. That morning he had felt prompted to call, and it was the very next day after we had given everything to God! The peace that overwhelmed us was amazing. God was again telling us that He saw everything, and He was still in control.

I began hearing about ways that diet and lifestyle changes can help fight cancer. A plan emerged, and I began to eat and live differently. After getting back home and recuperating a bit, we had another meeting with the doctor to talk about further treatment. By that time we felt the Lord was telling us not to do a transplant. But how would we say this to a doctor who had said I had only a twenty percent chance to live without a transplant? Many people were praying the morning I went for my appointment.

A doctor's words never sounded sweeter to me than his did that day. "We cannot find a match for you. But you seem to be doing so well that we recommend not doing the transplant, and just wait and see how things go," he said.

*Praise the Lord!* We felt released from a huge weight. We would continue with the course we felt the Lord had given us to follow. In addition, the doctors said I needed to stay off work for a year to let my body rest and recuperate and to try to avoid stress, a major factor in relapses.

So far I have continued to improve and my blood results have always been clear. It does not matter what may happen to my body, or what we may be called to go through. My faith is in a God who is much greater than we are. I must daily surrender myself to His will, and then I find the "peace of God, which passeth all understanding."

*Now unto him that is able to do exceeding abundantly above all that we ask or think, according to the power that worketh in us, unto him be glory. . . . Amen.*
Ephesians 3:20, 21

# Love Longings Fulfilled

*Vivian Benner*
*As told to Norma Plank*

In a family of nine, I was the third child. I attended a one-room school with about forty-five students and one teacher. I enjoyed school and wanted to someday be a first-grade teacher, but I only went through the eighth grade.

In our home we never had Bible reading or audible prayer at the table. In my late teens we began giving silent thanks for our food. We didn't always go to church. When Mom had Sunday dinner guests, which was often, she stayed home.

On our forty-two acre farm, we had a few Jersey cows, which gave us all the milk, cream, and butter our family needed. My father did custom butchering, and my mother baked and tended a booth at the farmer's market on Saturday mornings. I helped with baking and cleaned pig casings for stuffing sausages. Every Friday, my job was to make enough pie crumbs to fill a large dishpan, and then to make forty-five to fifty pies for the restaurant at the market. I still enjoy making pies.

But, for some reason, no matter what I did, I could never please my mother. Because I couldn't do things as well as my older sister, I was called lazy. Sometimes I was, I'm sure. I longed to be loved and appreciated. Finally I gave up.

I chose to be baptized at age seventeen because my girlfriends were taking that step, but I knew nothing of salvation. I hoped this would help my relationship with my mom. It didn't!

In my twenties I worked for two families, and both of these mothers appreciated and complimented me. This made a big difference in my life, and from then on, I found work more enjoyable.

I was very close to my sister, who was 3½ years younger than me. When we were on our own, we owned a house together and started a day nursery, taking care of children while their parents worked. It was a good business that continued for over four years. One day my sister said, "We're dissolving the partnership!" I was shocked. The only explanation she gave was, "I'll take all the blame."

At that time the ministers held me back from Communion because my oldest brother told them I was causing problems with my sister. I became discouraged and ended up changing churches. I felt that no one loved or cared for me. Though I was unaware of it, Someone did care deeply for me. I was incredibly ignorant of the Scriptures. How would God find me and show me His love? I have learned that God has many ways of contacting those who long for the love and rest that He alone can give.

After many job changes and living here and there, the Lord gave me a wake-up call through a dream when I was thirty-two. I dreamed the end of the world had come, and I was not ready. I woke up sweating and trembling, but the sad part was that I did not know how to get ready. The Lord saw my need and sent my aunt to show me the way. She helped me find salvation on September 13, 1959. Oh, what a happy day! I'm so thankful for God's mercy in keeping me until I found my way to Him.

The very next day I got busy making things right as He revealed things to me. Several years later God showed me more things that I needed to make right. What joy to have a clear conscience and Someone to always love me! God will never turn His back on me and tell me to go away.

Besides that, He blessed me with the love of two godly husbands. I married Seth Troyer in 1977, and we had six good years together before a heart attack took him in 1983. Then I married Paul Benner in 1989, and we enjoyed fourteen years together before cancer took him to his eternal home. For most of those years, Paul enjoyed good health, and we were able to do many things together.

One weekend, Paul and I were helping to cook at Sharon Mennonite Bible Institute. Again God blessed me with a wonderful dream. I saw a great light, and I knew

Jesus was coming. In joyous excitement, I grabbed Paul's arm and exclaimed, "Jesus is coming!" This was a great contrast to my first dream when I was not ready to meet the Lord.

God is so good!

Christian Light Publications, Inc., is a nonprofit, conservative Mennonite publishing company providing Christ-centered, Biblical literature including books, Gospel tracts, Sunday school materials, summer Bible school materials, and a full curriculum for Christian day schools and homeschools. Though produced primarily in English, some books, tracts, and school materials are also available in Spanish.

For more information about the ministry of CLP or its publications, or for spiritual help, please contact us at:

Christian Light Publications, Inc.
P. O. Box 1212
Harrisonburg, VA 22803-1212


Telephone—540-434-0768
Fax—540-433-8896
E-mail—info@clp.org
www.clp.org